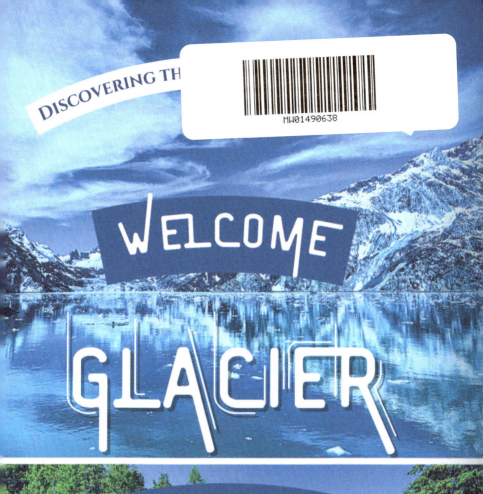

DISCOVERING TH

MW01490638

WELCOME

GLACIER

NATIONAL PARK

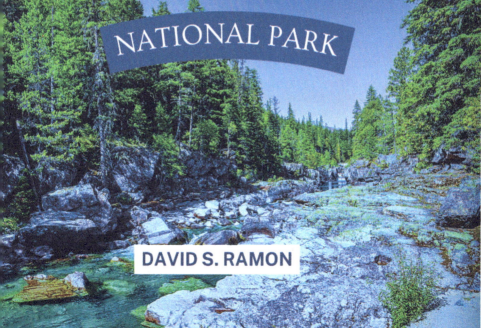

DAVID S. RAMON

Table of Contents

01
Introduction

02
Planning Your Visit

03
Getting There

04
Accommodations

GLACIER NATIONAL PARK MAP

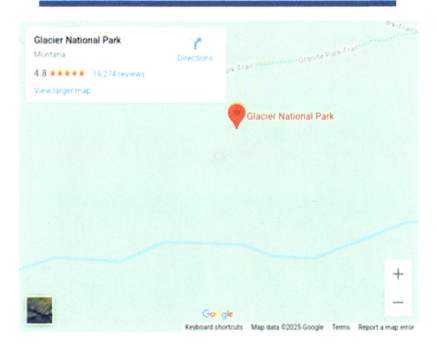

SCAN THE QR CODE

1. **Open Your Camera/Scanner App:** Most smartphones have a built-in QR scanner in the Camera app. If not, download a scanner app.
2. **Point at the QR Code:** Align the QR code within the camera frame and ensure it's well-lit.
3. **Hold Steady:** Wait for the device to recognize the code.
4. **Access the Content:** Tap the notification or link that appears to open or save the information.

THERE'S AN ENTIRE SECTION FILLED WITH INTERACTIVE MAPS

GOING-TO-THE-SUN MAP

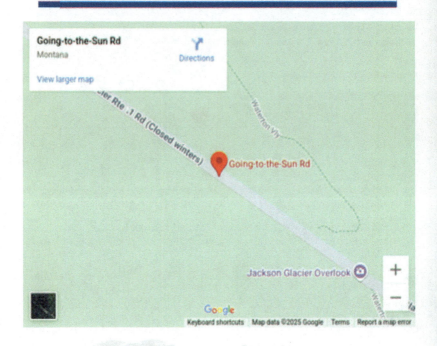

SCAN THE QR CODE

1. **Open Your Camera/Scanner App:** Most smartphones have a built-in QR scanner in the Camera app. If not, download a scanner app.
2. **Point at the QR Code:** Align the QR code within the camera frame and ensure it's well-lit.
3. **Hold Steady:** Wait for the device to recognize the code.
4. **Access the Content:** Tap the notification or link that appears to open or save the information.

THERE'S AN ENTIRE SECTION FILLED WITH INTERACTIVE MAPS

COPYRIGHT

AUTHOR PAGE

David S. Ramon is a seasoned travel writer and adventurer whose passion for exploration has taken him across the globe. With years of experience uncovering hidden gems, vibrant cultures, and breathtaking landscapes, David has dedicated his career to crafting immersive and practical travel guides that inspire and inform. Together with his team of seasoned travelers, photographers, and researchers, David has journeyed through bustling cities, remote islands, rugged mountain ranges, and pristine coastlines. From the vibrant street markets of Southeast Asia to the ancient ruins of South America, they have experienced the world firsthand, ensuring that every recommendation in his guides is authentic, insightful, and tailored for travelers of all kinds. David 's travel guides go beyond the typical tourist spots, offering in-depth cultural insights, local secrets, and practical tips that help travelers navigate new destinations with confidence. Whether you're an intrepid explorer or a first-time traveler, his books provide the tools to turn any journey into an unforgettable experience. Follow David S. Ramon and his team as they continue to explore new horizons, discovering the best the world has to offer—one destination at a time.

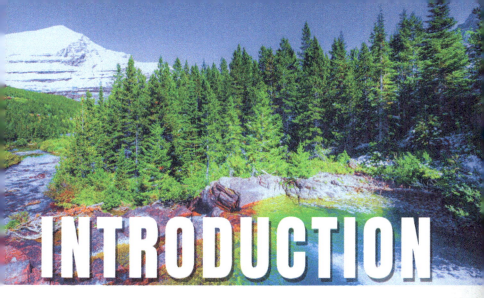

INTRODUCTION

Glacier National Park – Where the Wild Still Rules

There are few places left in the world where nature feels truly untamed—where jagged peaks rise like stone fortresses, where icy-blue lakes mirror the sky, and where the howl of wolves and the distant rumble of avalanches remind you that this land belongs to the wild. **Glacier National Park** is one of those places.

Tucked into the remote wilderness of northern Montana, along the Canadian border, Glacier is more than just a national park—it's a living, breathing testament to the raw power of nature. This million-acre wonderland, often called "The **Crown of the Continent**," is a land sculpted by ice and time. Towering summits, dense evergreen forests, and shimmering glacial lakes create a landscape so dramatic it seems almost unreal.

Over 130 named lakes reflect the surrounding peaks, and more than **700 miles of hiking trails** wind through alpine meadows, past waterfalls, and into the heart of some of the wildest backcountry in North America.

But this is not just a place to admire from a distance. **Glacier is an adventure waiting to happen.**

- Drive the legendary Going-to-the-Sun Road, an engineering marvel that clings to the cliffs and crosses the Continental Divide, offering one of the most breathtaking scenic drives in the world.
- Hike through fields of wildflowers, past hidden turquoise lakes, and up rocky switchbacks where mountain goats perch on ledges like sentinels of the peaks.
- Kayak across **Lake McDonald's** mirror-like surface at sunrise, when the mountains glow with the first light of day.
- Witness a grizzly bear fishing in a rushing river or a moose wading through a misty marsh at dawn.

- Stand beneath the towering waterfalls of Many Glacier, feeling the spray on your skin as the roar echoes through the valley.
- Camp beneath a sky so dark and clear that the Milky Way seems close enough to touch.

Glacier National Park is not for those who seek convenience. It's remote. It's rugged. It's unpredictable. Weather changes in an instant, wildlife wanders freely, and the mountains demand respect. But for those willing to embrace the adventure, Glacier offers something rare—a chance to step into the wilderness as it was meant to be.

66 What This Guide Offers 99

This comprehensive travel guide is designed to help you experience Glacier National Park at its fullest— whether you're here for a quick visit or a deep backcountry exploration. You'll find:

- **Insider tips on when to visit, how to get around, and where to stay** (from historic lodges to remote campgrounds).

- Detailed breakdowns of the park's best hikes, from easy scenic strolls to bucket-list summits.
- Expert advice on wildlife encounters, including bear safety and the best places to see moose, bighorn sheep, and more.
- Adventure recommendations beyond hiking—kayaking, fishing, horseback riding, and even winter excursions.
- Photography hotspots for capturing the park's most awe-inspiring views.
- Practical travel logistics, including permits, reservations, and packing essentials for every season.

Glacier is not just another national park. It is a sanctuary for the wild, a refuge for those seeking solitude, and a proving ground for adventurers. **This is a place where you don't just witness nature—you feel it, breathe it, and become part of it.**

So lace up your boots, pack your camera, and get ready for the journey of a lifetime. **Glacier is waiting.**

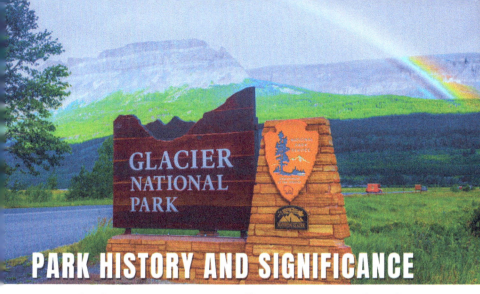

PARK HISTORY AND SIGNIFICANCE

A Land of Legacy: From Indigenous Homeland to Protected Wilderness

Long before Glacier National Park became a sanctuary for adventure seekers and nature lovers, it was—and remains—sacred land to the **Blackfeet, Salish, and Kootenai** tribes. For thousands of years, these Indigenous peoples lived in harmony with this rugged, untamed landscape, hunting bison on the plains, fishing in the crystal-clear lakes, and moving through the towering mountains with deep respect for the spirits that resided there. To the Blackfeet, who occupied the park's eastern side, the mountains were a sacred place known as the "Backbone of the World," a realm of spiritual power and ancestral wisdom. The Salish and Kootenai, whose lands stretched into the western valleys, traveled through the region for hunting and seasonal gathering, their lives deeply intertwined with the rhythms of the land.

Despite their long stewardship of this land, the late 19th century brought profound change. Treaties and forced removals pushed Indigenous nations from much of their traditional territory, making way for westward expansion. Yet, their cultural and spiritual ties to Glacier remain unbroken—today, the **Blackfeet Nation** still borders the park, and Indigenous history and perspectives are gaining long-overdue recognition in its interpretation and conservation efforts.

THE BIRTH OF A NATIONAL PARK

By the late 1800s, as the frontier era faded, a new appreciation for America's wild places took hold. One of the earliest champions of Glacier's preservation was George Bird Grinnell, a naturalist, writer, and conservationist who had long admired the region's dramatic peaks, pristine lakes, and diverse wildlife. After years of lobbying, his efforts bore fruit: on May 11, 1910, Glacier National Park was officially established, becoming the 10th national park in the United States. From its inception, Glacier was a place of pioneering spirit. Visitors arrived by Great Northern Railway, which played a key role in promoting the park as the "Switzerland of America," constructing rustic yet grand lodges and chalets to welcome travelers.

But while human footprints began to grow, the park remained first and foremost a haven for wildlife, home to grizzly bears, mountain goats, moose, and wolverines.

THE CROWN OF THE CONTINENT

Glacier National Park is more than just a breathtaking landscape—it is part of a greater ecological masterpiece. Together with Canada's Waterton Lakes National Park, it forms the Waterton-Glacier International Peace Park, established in 1932 as the world's first International Peace Park, symbolizing cross-border conservation. This vast, interconnected wilderness is known as the Crown of the Continent Ecosystem, a region spanning over 18 million acres of mountains, forests, rivers, and prairies.

Because of its extraordinary biodiversity and pristine landscapes, Glacier has earned global recognition:

- In 1976, it was designated a UNESCO Biosphere Reserve, acknowledging its role in scientific research, conservation, and sustainable tourism.
- In 1995, it was named a UNESCO World Heritage Site, joining the ranks of Earth's most treasured natural wonders.

A LIVING LEGACY OF CONSERVATION

Glacier's history is not just about its past—it's about its ongoing protection. Climate change poses a stark challenge: when the park was founded in 1910, it had **over 150 glaciers**. Today, fewer than **25 remain**, and scientists predict that within a few decades, the park may lose them entirely. Yet Glacier remains a powerful symbol of resilience. Conservationists, Indigenous leaders, park rangers, and visitors all play a role in protecting this extraordinary place.

Every time you step onto a trail, gaze across a valley sculpted by ice, or watch a grizzly roam the wildflower meadows, you are witnessing a landscape shaped by millennia of history, culture, and conservation efforts. Glacier National Park is more than just a destination—it's a testament to the power of preservation, a reminder that some places should remain wild, untamed, and free for generations to come.

PLANNING YOUR VISIT

Best Times to Visit Glacier National Park

Glacier National Park is a land of shifting moods —snow-capped and silent in winter, bursting with life in spring, golden and crisp in autumn, and buzzing with adventure in summer. When you visit will shape your experience, from the trails you can access to the wildlife you might encounter.

Summer (June – September): Peak Season & Prime Access

Summer is Glacier's busiest season, and for good reason: it's when the park is fully open, with most roads, trails, and lodges accessible. The legendary Going-to-the-Sun Road, which crosses the Continental Divide and offers some of the most breathtaking views in North America, typically opens by late June or early July, depending on snow levels.

- Weather: Daytime highs range from 60°F to 80°F (15°C to 27°C), with cooler nights.
- Crowds: Expect heavy visitation, especially in July and August—parking lots at popular trailheads like Logan Pass and Many Glacier fill early. Reservations are required for certain areas, including Going-to-the-Sun Road.
- Wildlife: Summer is prime time for grizzly and black bear sightings, especially in the high country. Mountain goats and bighorn sheep frequent the alpine areas, and moose can be spotted in wetlands.

- Hiking & Outdoor Activities: With over 700 miles of trails, summer is the best time for hiking, backpacking, and kayaking. Wildflowers peak in mid-to-late July, transforming valleys into a vibrant sea of purple lupines, red Indian paintbrush, and yellow glacier lilies.
- Events: Ranger-led programs, night sky events, and the Waterton-Glacier International Peace Park Assembly (held in alternating years) add to the experience.

Fall (September – October): Golden Larches & Tranquility

As summer fades, Glacier transforms into a quieter, golden-hued wonderland. By mid-September, crowds thin, lodging becomes more available, and the park takes on a peaceful beauty.

- Weather: Crisp and cool, with highs in the 50s and 60s°F (10–20°C). Nights can dip below freezing, and early snow is possible by October.
- Crowds: Fewer visitors make for a more serene experience, especially in late September.
- Wildlife: Fall is rutting season for elk and bighorn sheep, meaning dramatic wildlife encounters. Bears are actively foraging before hibernation, making it one of the best times for sightings.
- Foliage: Golden larch trees (a rarity in North America) set the mountainsides ablaze with color from late September to mid-October, especially in the Many Glacier and Two Medicine areas.
- Hiking & Road Access: Most trails remain open, but snow can arrive unexpectedly. Going-to-the-Sun Road is typically open until mid-October, though portions may close earlier.

📍 Best for: Photographers, wildlife enthusiasts, and those looking to experience Glacier in solitude.

SPRING (APRIL – JUNE): A PARK AWAKENING

Spring is Glacier's secret season—quiet, moody, and filled with the first signs of life. Snowmelt fuels roaring waterfalls, wildlife emerges from hibernation, and valleys turn lush with fresh greenery.

- Weather: Unpredictable. Temperatures range from 40°F to 60°F (4–16°C), but snow lingers in higher elevations well into June.
- Crowds: Minimal—you'll have trails and viewpoints to yourself. Lodges and park services begin reopening in late May.
- Wildlife: Bears are most active in spring, often seen in lower elevations. Elk and deer give birth to their young, making it a great time for wildlife spotting.
- Hiking & Road Access: Many low-elevation trails open by May, but most alpine trails remain snow-covered until mid-to-late June. Going-to-the-Sun Road partially opens in late spring, but full access isn't guaranteed until late June or early July.

📌 **Best for: Wildlife lovers, solitude seekers, and those who don't mind a little unpredictability.**

Winter (November – March): A Frozen Wilderness

Glacier in winter is a world transformed—silent, snow-draped, and utterly wild. While most of the park shuts down, those who brave the cold are rewarded with jaw-dropping winter scenery and solitude.

- Weather: Cold, with highs in the 20s and 30s°F (-6 to 3°C). Heavy snowfall is common.
- Crowds: Almost none. You'll have the park's vast landscapes nearly to yourself.
- Wildlife: Moose, bighorn sheep, and snow-dusted bison can be seen, but bears are hibernating.
- Activities: Snowshoeing, cross-country skiing, and backcountry winter camping in designated areas.
- Road Access: Going-to-the-Sun Road is closed beyond Lake McDonald Lodge, but the Apgar and West Glacier areas remain open.

ENTRANCE FEES AND PASSES

Planning a visit to Glacier National Park requires understanding the entrance fees, available passes, and reservation systems to ensure a seamless experience. Here's a detailed breakdown:

Entrance Fees

Glacier National Park charges entrance fees based on the mode of transportation, with rates varying between peak and off-peak seasons:

- Private Vehicle: $35.00 per vehicle, valid for seven consecutive days. During the winter season (November 1 to April 30), the fee is reduced to $25.00.
- Motorcycle: $30.00 per motorcycle, also valid for seven days. The winter rate is $20.00.
- Per Person: Individuals entering on foot, bicycle, or as part of a non-commercial group are charged $20.00 per person, with a reduced rate of $15.00 during winter.

Please note that the park operates on a cashless system; only credit or debit card payments are accepted.

Annual and Interagency Passes

For visitors planning multiple trips or exploring other federal recreation areas, the following passes offer value:

- Glacier National Park Annual Pass: Priced at $70.00, this pass provides unlimited entry to Glacier National Park for one year from the month of purchase.
- America the Beautiful – National Parks and Federal Recreational Lands Annual Pass: At $80.00, this pass grants access to more than 2,000 federal recreation sites, including all national parks, for one year. It's ideal for travelers visiting multiple parks within a year.

Discounted Passes

Several discounted or free passes are available for eligible individuals:

- Senior Pass: Available to U.S. citizens or permanent residents aged 62 or older. An annual Senior Pass is $20.00, while a lifetime pass is $80.00.
- Military Pass: A free annual pass for current U.S. military members and their dependents, as well as veterans and Gold Star Families.
- Access Pass: A free lifetime pass for U.S. citizens or permanent residents with permanent disabilities.

- 4th Grade Pass: A free annual pass for U.S. 4th graders (or equivalent homeschoolers) and their families, valid from September through August of the student's 4th-grade year.

These passes can be obtained online through the USGS Online Store or at the park's entrance stations.

Vehicle Reservations

To manage traffic and enhance visitor experience during peak season, Glacier National Park implements a vehicle reservation system for certain areas:

- Going-to-the-Sun Road (West Entrance): From June 13 through September 28, 2025, vehicle reservations are required between 7am and 3pm Visitors can enter without a reservation before 7 a.m. or after 3 p.m.
- North Fork Area: The same reservation requirements and dates apply as for the Going-to-the-Sun Road.

Reservations can be made via Recreation.gov and are released in two phases:

- Advanced Reservations: Available 120 days in advance on a rolling basis, starting February 13 at 8 a.m. Mountain Time.
- Next-Day Reservations: Released daily at 7 p.m. Mountain Time for entry the following day, beginning June 12, 2025.

It's important to note that a vehicle reservation is separate from the park entrance fee. Visitors must have both a valid entrance pass and a vehicle reservation to access these areas during the specified times.

Free Entrance Days

The National Park Service designates several fee-free days each year, allowing visitors to enjoy national parks without paying an entrance fee. While the specific dates for 2025 have not been announced yet, they often include:

- Martin Luther King Jr. Day (January)
- National Park Week (April)
- Great American Outdoors Act Anniversary (August)
- National Public Lands Day (September)
- Veterans Day (November)

These fee-free days can be an excellent opportunity to visit Glacier National Park, though it's advisable to arrive early, as they tend to attract larger crowds.

PARK REGULATIONS AND SAFETY TIPS

To preserve the natural beauty and ecological balance of **Glacier National Park**, visitors must adhere to key regulations:

- **Campfire Restrictions:** Campfires are only permitted in designated fire rings at front-country campgrounds.

- **Campfire Restrictions:** Campfires are only permitted in designated fire rings at front-country campgrounds. Fire bans may be enforced during dry conditions to prevent wildfires—always check current fire regulations before lighting a fire.
- **Wildlife Protection Laws:** Do not feed, approach, or harass wildlife. Keep a minimum distance of **100 yards from bears and wolves** and **25 yards from all other animals**. Violating these rules can result in fines and endanger both visitors and wildlife.
- **Leave No Trace Principles:** Pack out all trash, stay on designated trails, and minimize human impact. Avoid picking plants, disturbing rock formations, or creating new trails.
- **Backcountry Permit Requirements:** Any overnight stay in the **backcountry** requires a **backcountry camping permit**, which can be obtained through the National Park Service website or at visitor centers. Some high-demand routes require early reservations.
- **Drones & Off-Road Vehicles:** Drone use is strictly prohibited in the park, and off-road driving is not allowed.

Safety Tips for Hiking, Camping, and Wildlife Encounters

Hiking Safety

- **Carry Bear Spray** and know how to use it—encounters with grizzly and black bears are common.
- **Hike in Groups:** Solo hiking increases risks. Travel in groups of **three or more** for safety.
- **Make Noise:** Call out, clap, or use bear bells when hiking to avoid surprising animals.
- **Check Trail Conditions:** Some trails may be closed due to wildlife activity, snow, or rockslides.

Camping Safety

- **Proper Food Storage:** Store all food, trash, and scented items in **bear-proof lockers** or hang them from bear poles at backcountry campsites.
- **Camp Away from Water Sources:** To minimize wildlife encounters, set up camp at least **200 feet from lakes and streams**.
- **Prepare for Cold Nights:** Even in summer, nighttime temperatures can drop below freezing, so bring proper gear.

WILDLIFE ENCOUNTER SAFETY

- **Bears:** If you encounter a bear, **stay calm, do not run.** Slowly back away while speaking calmly. If the bear approaches, **stand your ground, use bear spray if necessary.**
- **Mountain Lions:** Maintain eye contact, make yourself appear larger, and back away slowly—never turn your back.
- **Moose:** Give moose plenty of space and avoid getting between a mother and her calf. They can be aggressive if threatened.

Weather Preparedness & Natural Hazards

- **Sudden Weather Changes:** Temperatures and weather conditions change rapidly—always carry **rain gear, warm layers, and extra food and water**.
- **Road Closures: Going-to-the-Sun Road** and other high-elevation routes may close due to snow, rockslides, or maintenance—check with the park service before planning your drive.
- **Avalanche Risks:** If hiking in winter or early spring, be aware of **avalanche-prone areas**. Always check avalanche forecasts before venturing into backcountry terrain.
- **Lightning Safety:** In alpine areas, thunderstorms can develop quickly. If caught in a storm, descend from ridges and seek shelter away from lone trees and exposed areas.

EMERGENCY CONTACTS

- **Park Headquarters:** (406) 888-7800
- **Emergency (24/7): Dial 911** for immediate assistance.
- **Ranger Stations:** Available at Apgar, St. Mary, and Many Glacier for information and aid.

- **Weather & Road Updates:** Call (406) 888-7800 or visit the **National Park Service website** for current conditions.

Pet Regulations

- **Pets are restricted** to developed areas, front-country campgrounds, and paved roads—they are **not allowed on hiking trails or in backcountry areas** to protect wildlife.
- Dogs must be **leashed (6 feet max)** at all times.
- Never leave pets unattended in vehicles due to extreme temperature fluctuations.
- Consider using **Glacier National Park's nearby pet boarding services** if you plan to hike extensively.

GETTING THERE

G lacier National Park, a crown jewel of the Northern Rockies, offers multiple entry points, each leading to distinct regions of the park. Whether you arrive by car, train, or plane, planning your route in advance is essential, especially given the park's seasonal road closures and remote location.

Main Entry Points to Glacier National Park

Glacier National Park has seven main entrances, but four are the most commonly used by visitors:

1. West Glacier Entrance (Main Entrance)
    - Located near West Glacier, Montana, this is the most popular and accessible gateway to the park.
    - Provides direct access to Going-to-the-Sun Road, Lake McDonald, Apgar Village, and many visitor services.

- Closest entry point to Glacier Park International Airport (FCA) and the Amtrak Empire Builder train route.

2. St. Mary Entrance (East Side)

- The eastern counterpart to West Glacier, located in St. Mary, Montana.
- Ideal for accessing the eastern portion of Going-to-the-Sun Road and St. Mary Lake.
- Provides easy access to Many Glacier and Two Medicine areas.

3. Many Glacier Entrance (Northeast Side)

- A scenic but less-visited entrance leading to **Many Glacier Valley**, home to stunning landscapes, hiking trails, and the iconic **Many Glacier Hotel**.
- Accessible via **U.S. Highway 89** and **Route 3 (Many Glacier Road)** from St. Mary.

4. Two Medicine Entrance (Southeast Side)

- Located near the town of East Glacier Park, this quieter entrance leads to Two Medicine Lake, a remote and breathtaking area with excellent hiking and scenic boat tours.
- Offers quick access to East Glacier Park Village, which has an Amtrak station.

Getting to Glacier National Park by Car

Driving is the most common way to reach Glacier National Park, offering flexibility and the ability to explore the region at your own pace. The park is best accessed via U.S. Highway 2, U.S. Highway 89, and Montana Highway 49.

- From Kalispell, MT: ~45 minutes to West Glacier (via U.S. Highway 2).
- From Missoula, MT: ~2.5 hours to West Glacier (via U.S. Highway 93 & MT-206).
- From Great Falls, MT: ~3 hours to St. Mary (via U.S. Highway 89).
- From Bozeman, MT: ~5 hours to West Glacier (via I-90 & U.S. Highway 2).
- From Calgary, Canada: ~4 hours to St. Mary (via AB-2 & U.S. Highway 89).

🚗 Rental Cars & Road Conditions

Car rentals are available in Kalispell, Missoula, Great Falls, and nearby towns. However, note that Going-to-the-Sun Road has vehicle size restrictions (21 feet long, 8 feet wide, 10 feet tall).

🚦 **Seasonal Closures:** Many park roads, including Going-to-the-Sun Road, are closed in winter and typically open from late June to early October, depending on snowfall.

Getting to Glacier National Park by plane

The nearest airport to Glacier National Park is Glacier Park International Airport (FCA) in Kalispell, Montana. Other regional airports offer alternative routes.

✈️ Nearest Airports:

1. Glacier Park International Airport (FCA) – 30 miles from West Glacier
   - Direct flights from major U.S. cities, including Denver, Seattle, Salt Lake City, and Chicago.
   - Car rentals, shuttles, and taxis available.
2. Missoula Montana Airport (MSO) – 150 miles from West Glacier
   - A larger airport with more flight options. Best for travelers combining Glacier with a road trip.

3. Great Falls International Airport (GTF) – 130 miles from St. Mary

   ○ Convenient for accessing the eastern side of the park.

4. Calgary International Airport (YYC), Canada – 200 miles from St. Mary

   ○ Ideal for travelers from Canada, offering a scenic drive through Alberta into Montana.

Seasonal Access & Road Closures

Due to its high elevation and rugged terrain, Glacier National Park has significant **seasonal road closures**:

🔴 **Going-to-the-Sun Road:**

- **Closed in winter** (typically from mid-October to late June).
- Open fully from **late June to early October**, but exact dates depend on snow removal.
- A **Vehicle Reservation System** is often required for summer visits.

🔴 **Many Glacier Road:**

- Open from **mid-May to mid-October** but subject to snow and maintenance delays.
- 🔴 Two Medicine & North Fork Areas:
- Access is limited in winter, with most roads unplowed.
- 🚗 Winter Access:
- West Glacier Entrance remains open year-round, but visitors can only drive as far as Lake McDonald Lodge.

Getting Around Glacier National Park

Once inside Glacier National Park, visitors have a variety of ways to explore its rugged landscapes, from driving the iconic **Going-to-the-Sun Road** to taking advantage of park shuttles, guided tours, and even biking or horseback riding. The right transportation choice depends on your itinerary, comfort level, and desire for adventure.

🚗 Rental Cars & Personal Vehicles

For most visitors, **driving your own or a rental car** is the most flexible way to navigate the park. Glacier's vast wilderness spans over a million acres, and while some areas are accessible by shuttle or guided tours, having your own vehicle allows for a more customized experience.

Where to Rent a Car

- **Glacier Park International Airport (FCA)** – The closest airport, located in Kalispell, has rental car options from major companies like Hertz, Enterprise, and Alamo.
- **Whitefish, MT** – A popular gateway town with rental services, especially convenient for Amtrak travelers.
- **West Glacier & East Glacier** – A few local rental agencies operate here, but availability is limited.

Considerations for Driving in the Park

- Going-to-the-Sun Road Restrictions: Vehicles over 21 feet long, 8 feet wide, or 10 feet tall are not allowed due to narrow lanes and tight turns.
- Parking Challenges: Popular areas like Logan Pass and Avalanche Lake fill up early (often by 8 AM in summer).
- Gas Stations: There are no gas stations inside the park, so fill up in West Glacier, St. Mary, or East Glacier before entering.

🚗 Best For: Travelers who want freedom to explore at their own pace and reach less-accessible areas like Many Glacier, Two Medicine, and the North Fork.

🚌 Glacier National Park Shuttle System

One of the best ways to experience Glacier without the hassle of parking is by using the Glacier National Park Shuttle System. This free shuttle service operates along Going-to-the-Sun Road, providing a convenient way to hop between key locations while enjoying the scenery stress-free.

Shuttle Routes & Stops

- West Side Shuttle (Apgar to Logan Pass)
  - Key Stops: Apgar Visitor Center, Lake McDonald Lodge, Avalanche Creek, The Loop, Logan Pass
- East Side Shuttle (St. Mary to Logan Pass)
  - Key Stops: St. Mary Visitor Center, Rising Sun, Siyeh Bend, Logan Pass
- Logan Pass Connection (Links east and west routes)
  - Logan Pass serves as the main hub, where passengers switch between the east and west routes.

Schedule & Frequency

- Operates early July to mid-September, depending on road conditions.
- Runs approximately every 15–30 minutes at major stops.
- First shuttles start at 7:00 AM from Apgar and St. Mary Visitor Centers.
- Last shuttles leave Logan Pass around 5:00–6:00 PM.

Shuttle Cost

- Completely FREE with park entrance!

Pros & Cons of Taking the Shuttle

✅ Pros:

- No need to worry about parking in busy areas.
- Great for hikers doing point-to-point trails (e.g., Highline Trail, Hidden Lake, Siyeh Pass).
- Eco-friendly and a fantastic way to take in the views while letting someone else drive.

❌ Cons:

- Seats fill up fast, especially at Logan Pass, so expect wait times of 30+ minutes in peak summer.
- Doesn't serve Many Glacier, Two Medicine, or North Fork areas.
- Not ideal for those wanting to stop frequently for photos.

🚌 Best For: Travelers who don't want to deal with parking headaches, solo hikers doing one-way treks, and anyone looking for a budget-friendly option.

🚌 Guided Tours & Private Shuttles

If you want to learn more about the park from local experts, **guided tours** and **private shuttles** offer a comfortable and informative alternative.

1. Red Bus Tours – 🏔 A Classic Glacier Experience

- Operated by **Glacier National Park Lodges**, the **Red Jammer Buses** have been giving tours since the 1930s!
- Drivers, known as **Jammers**, provide entertaining and informative commentary.
- **Popular Routes:**
    - **Going-to-the-Sun Road Full Tour** (West Glacier to St. Mary and back)
    - **Many Glacier & Two Medicine Scenic Tours**
    - **Sunset and Photography Tours**

📍 **Cost:** ~$60-$120 per person (varies by tour length).

🔶 **Reservations Required:** Book early, as these tours **sell out months in advance**.

2. Sun Tours – 🌿 Blackfeet Cultural Perspective

- Led by members of the **Blackfeet Nation**, offering unique insights into the park's Indigenous history.
- Covers major areas like **Going-to-the-Sun Road, Many Glacier, and Two Medicine**.

📍 **Cost:** ~$80-$100 per person.

3. Xanterra Shuttles & Private Tour Operators

- Private shuttle services offer **custom tours and transportation** to Many Glacier and beyond.
- Companies like **Glacier Adventure Guides** offer **hiking shuttles** to remote trailheads.

🚐 **Best For:** Visitors who want an **educational, relaxing** experience or those without a car who need **direct rides** to less accessible parts of the park.

🚴 Biking in Glacier National Park

For active travelers, biking offers an unforgettable way to experience the park—especially in early summer, when Going-to-the-Sun Road is still closed to cars but open to cyclists!

Best Biking Routes:

🚴 Going-to-the-Sun Road (Before Cars Allowed)

- Late May to mid-June: Cyclists have the road almost to themselves before it opens to vehicles.
- Most Popular Stretch: Avalanche Creek to Logan Pass (steep but rewarding).

🚴 Apgar to West Glacier & Lake McDonald

- A scenic, mostly flat ride with gorgeous lake views.

🚴 Many Glacier Road & Camas Road

- Less crowded but still offers stunning mountain scenery

📍 **Bike Rentals Available in:**

- **West Glacier, Apgar Village, and Whitefish.**

🚵 **Best For:** Active travelers looking for a **unique way** to explore Glacier's breathtaking landscapes.

🐎 **Horseback Riding**

Experience Glaciers **like early explorers did**—on horseback! Several outfitters offer guided rides through scenic valleys and forests.

Best Places for Horseback Riding:

- **Apgar & Lake McDonald Area** – Family-friendly, short rides through beautiful forests.
- **Many Glaciers** – Stunning alpine scenery with a high chance of spotting wildlife.
- **Two Medicine** – A more **off-the-beaten-path** horseback riding experience.

Horseback Outfitters:

🐎 **Swan Mountain Outfitters** – Official provider within the park.

🐎 **Glacier Gateway Trail Rides** – Offers scenic rides just outside the park.

📍 **Cost:** ~$75-$150 per person, depending on ride length.

🕐 **Rides range from 1-hour gentle loops to full-day wilderness adventures.**

🐎 **Best For:** Travelers who want a **relaxing, scenic** experience while exploring the park's trails.

Navigating Glacier National Park: Maps and Routes

Glacier National Park is a vast wilderness with breathtaking mountain passes, glacial valleys, and pristine lakes—much of it accessible only by a few key roads. Knowing the best routes and how to navigate them is crucial for a smooth trip. Below, we cover the park's most famous roads, the best sources for maps and navigation tools, and important tips on dealing with limited cell service.

🚗 Key Roads in Glacier National Park

1. Going-to-the-Sun Road – 🏞️ The Crown Jewel of Glacier

⛰️ What It Offers:

- One of the most famous scenic drives in North America, Going-to-the-Sun Road (GTTSR) stretches 50 miles from West Glacier to St. Mary, crossing the Continental Divide at Logan Pass (6,646 feet).
- Jaw-dropping views of glacial valleys, waterfalls, alpine tundra, and rugged peaks.
- Access to Logan Pass Visitor Center, Hidden Lake Overlook, Highline Trail, and Avalanche Lake.

🛣️ Difficulty Level:

- 🚗 Moderate – Paved but narrow, winding, and steep in places.
- 🚫 Large Vehicle Restrictions: Vehicles longer than 21 feet, wider than 8 feet, or taller than 10 feet are prohibited beyond Avalanche Creek (west side) and Rising Sun (east side).
- 🚦 Best Time to Drive:
- Open fully from late June to early October (weather-dependent).
- Early morning (before 8 AM) or late afternoon (after 5 PM) to avoid traffic.
- Sunset drives are magical, offering golden light on the mountains.
- 🔴 Seasonal Closures:
- The road is closed to vehicles in winter, typically from mid-October to late June.
- In spring, portions are open to bicyclists and hikers before vehicles are allowed.
- 📌 Pro Tip: Start at West Glacier for the best gradual scenic buildup. If coming from St. Mary, you'll get the dramatic views immediately.

2. Many Glacier Road – 🏞️ A Gateway to the Park's Best Hikes

🚙 What It Offers:

- A 12-mile scenic drive from Babb, Montana into Many Glacier Valley, home to some of the park's best hikes and wildlife viewing.
- Access to Grinnell Glacier, Iceberg Lake, and Swiftcurrent Pass Trails.
- Bears, moose, and mountain goats are commonly seen.

🛣️ Difficulty Level:

- 🚗 Easy to Moderate – Paved but rough in sections due to frequent potholes.
- 🚦 Best Time to Drive:
  - Open from mid-May to mid-October.
  - Best visited early in the morning to avoid congestion and increase wildlife spotting chances.
  - Afternoon winds can make the lakes choppy, so morning boat tours are ideal.

📌 Pro Tip: If you want a quieter, early morning experience, stay at Many Glacier Hotel or Swiftcurrent Motor Inn the night before.

3. North Fork Road – 🌲 Off-the-Beaten-Path Adventure

🚙 What It Offers:

- A rugged, gravel road leading to the remote North Fork area, including Polebridge, Bowman Lake, and Kintla Lake.
- Spectacular wilderness, fewer crowds, and incredible solitude.
- Access to rustic Polebridge Mercantile, famous for its huckleberry bear claws!

🛣️ Difficulty Level:

- 🚙 Challenging – Unpaved, bumpy, and not recommended for low-clearance vehicles.
- 4WD or AWD is highly recommended during wet conditions.
- 🚦 Best Time to Drive:
  - Open from mid-May to mid-October.
  - Early morning or late afternoon to enjoy wildlife sightings and fewer vehicles.
  - Avoid after heavy rain, as the road can become slick and difficult to navigate.

📌 Pro Tip: Bring extra water, snacks, and a spare tire—services are limited, and road conditions can change quickly.

🗺 Best Maps & Navigation Tools

1. Official Glacier National Park Maps (FREE)

- 📍 Available At:
  - Park Entrance Stations – Free paper maps provided with your entrance fee.
  - Visitor Centers (Apgar, St. Mary, Logan Pass) – Larger, detailed maps available for reference.
  - Online – Downloadable PDFs from the National Park Service website.

📌 Pro Tip: Pick up a topographic hiking map from Apgar or St. Mary Visitor Centers if you plan on backcountry adventures.

2. NPS App (National Park Service App) 📱

- Free app with detailed maps, trail info, and road status updates.
- Works offline if maps are downloaded in advance.

✅ Best For: Real-time alerts on road closures, shuttle schedules, and ranger-led programs.

📌 Pro Tip: Before entering the park, download offline maps since cell service is unreliable.

3. AllTrails App 🥾

- Best for hiking route planning, with GPS tracking and difficulty ratings.
- Premium version allows offline access, perfect for Glacier's remote trails.

✅ Best For: Hikers who want real-time elevation data, trail reviews, and downloadable offline maps.

📌 Pro Tip: Look for recent trail reviews to check for wildlife sightings or trail conditions.

4. Gaia GPS & Maps.me 🦋

- Gaia GPS: Great for backcountry navigation, with detailed topographic maps.
- Maps.me: Offers offline road navigation, helpful if driving to remote areas.

📌 Pro Tip: Download the full Montana region before your trip for reliable offline access.

📶 Cell Service Limitations & Offline Navigation

🛰️ Cell Reception in Glacier is Extremely Limited.

- No service in Logan Pass, Many Glacier, North Fork, or Two Medicine.
- Some signal in West Glacier, St. Mary, Apgar Village, and East Glacier.
- Verizon and AT&T have the best coverage, but even these are spotty.

🛠 Tips for Staying Connected Without Cell Service

✅ Download Offline Maps & Apps Before Entering the Park.

✅ Print a Paper Map as a backup.

✅ Carry a GPS Device if venturing into remote areas.

✅ Let someone know your itinerary if hiking in isolated regions.

📌 Pro Tip: Visitor Centers have Wi-Fi hotspots where you can quickly download updated info if needed.

Final Thoughts: Best Way to Navigate the Park?

- 🚗 Drive for flexibility, but arrive early to beat parking congestion.
- 🚌 Use the Park Shuttle if exploring Going-to-the-Sun Road and want to avoid parking stress.
- 📱 Download Offline Maps (NPS App, AllTrails, or Gaia GPS) before your trip.
- 🗺 Carry a Paper Map as a backup—technology isn't always reliable here!

ACCESSIBILITY INFORMATION

Glacier National Park is known for its rugged terrain and remote wilderness, but it also offers several accessible features to ensure visitors of all abilities can experience its breathtaking landscapes. From scenic overlooks and wheelchair-friendly trails to accessible visitor centers and lodging, the park provides thoughtful accommodations for travelers with mobility challenges. Below, you'll find detailed information on accessible trails, services, lodging, and key accessibility resources to help plan your visit.

🏔 Wheelchair-Accessible Trails & Scenic Areas
While much of Glacier's terrain is steep and rugged, several paved or hard-packed gravel trails offer stunning views without difficult elevation changes.
1. Apgar Village & Lake McDonald Overlook 🌊
📍 Location: Apgar Village, near the West Entrance
  • Fully paved and wheelchair-friendly.
  • Offers expansive views of Lake McDonald and the surrounding peaks.
  • Nearby picnic areas and accessible restrooms.
  • Apgar Village also has accessible shops, restaurants, and the Apgar Visitor Center.

2. Trail of the Cedars 🌲

📍 Location: Off Going-to-the-Sun Road, near Avalanche Creek

- 0.9-mile boardwalk loop through an ancient cedar forest.
- One of the only wheelchair-accessible trails in the park.
- Features a scenic bridge over Avalanche Creek and stunning greenery.
- Accessible parking available at the trailhead.

3. Running Eagle Falls Trail 🏞️

📍 Location: Two Medicine Area (Southeast Glacier)

- 0.6-mile round-trip trail with a hard-packed surface, making it suitable for wheelchairs.
- Leads to Running Eagle Falls, a beautiful waterfall that flows through a rock formation.
- Accessible restrooms and picnic areas nearby.

4. St. Mary Lake Overlooks 🌅

📍 Location: East side of Glacier, near St. Mary Entrance

- Several roadside pullouts and short paved paths provide panoramic views of St. Mary Lake and Wild Goose Island.
- Easy access to photo spots without hiking.
- St. Mary Visitor Center also offers ADA-accessible exhibits and restrooms.

📌 Pro Tip: If you want incredible views with minimal walking, the Jackson Glacier Overlook on Going-to-the-Sun Road is wheelchair-accessible and offers one of the best glacier views in the park.

⛺ Accessible Lodging & Accommodations

Several Glacier National Park lodges, campgrounds, and hotels offer accessible rooms, entrances, and amenities. Inside the Park

🏨 Many Glacier Hotel (Many Glacier Area)

- Offers accessible rooms with roll-in showers.
- Elevators, paved paths, and accessible dining options.
- Beautiful views of Swiftcurrent Lake right from the lodge's decks.

🏨 Lake McDonald Lodge (West Side, Near Apgar)

- Wheelchair-accessible ground-floor rooms available.
- Paved walkways to Lake McDonald shoreline, the lodge dining area, and boat docks.
- Assistance available for boarding boat tours.

🏕 Accessible Campgrounds

- Apgar Campground (West Glacier) – Designated accessible campsites available.
- Rising Sun Campground (East Side) – Paved paths to restrooms and camp areas.
- Fish Creek Campground (Near Apgar) – Offers an ADA-compliant campsite and restroom.

📌 Pro Tip: Lodges inside Glacier National Park fill up quickly, so book accessible rooms at least 6-12 months in advance.

🚌 Accessibility on Going-to-the-Sun Road & Park Shuttles

Going-to-the-Sun Road Scenic Drive 🚙
- The entire 50-mile drive offers multiple scenic pullouts with accessible parking.
- Wheelchair-friendly viewpoints include:

✅ Lake McDonald Lodge

✅ Logan Pass Visitor Center (has ramps and accessible restrooms)

✅ Wild Goose Island Overlook

✅ Jackson Glacier Overlook

Glacier National Park Shuttle System 🚌
- The park's free shuttle has ADA-compliant vehicles on Going-to-the-Sun Road.
- All shuttles are equipped with wheelchair lifts and priority seating.
- Stops at Apgar, Avalanche Creek, The Loop, Logan Pass, and St. Mary Visitor Center.
- Best Use Case: Perfect for visitors who don't want to drive or need assistance getting to high-altitude locations like Logan Pass.

📍 Pro Tip: Not all stops have paved boarding areas—ask at visitor centers for best boarding locations.

♿ NPS Access Pass & Accessibility Services

🆓 America the Beautiful – Access Pass

- The National Park Service (NPS) Access Pass is a free lifetime pass for U.S. citizens with permanent disabilities.
- Covers entrance fees to Glacier and all other national parks.
- Provides discounts on campground fees.

📍 How to Get It:

- Available at Glacier entrance stations or apply online through the National Park Service website.

◆ Additional Accessibility Services

- Visitor Centers:
  - Apgar, St. Mary, and Logan Pass offer ADA-accessible restrooms, ramps, and exhibits.
- Ranger-Led Programs:
  - Some tours include assistive listening devices and wheelchair-friendly locations.
- Boat Tours:
  - Many Glacier and Lake McDonald offer assistance for boarding.
- Service Animals:
  - Permitted throughout the park, including trails and buildings.

📌 Pro Tip: Contact (406) 888-7800 (Glacier's park office) before visiting to confirm accessibility needs.

🅿 Accessible Parking & Restrooms

🚗 Accessible Parking Locations:
- Apgar Visitor Center
- Logan Pass Visitor Center
- Many Glacier Hotel & Swiftcurrent Motor Inn
- Lake McDonald Lodge
- St. Mary Visitor Center

🚻 Accessible Restrooms Available At:
- All visitor centers (Apgar, St. Mary, Logan Pass).
- Major lodges (Many Glacier, Lake McDonald, Rising Sun).
- Avalanche Picnic Area and Trail of the Cedars trailhead.

📌 Pro Tip: Most accessible restrooms are located near major parking areas—smaller trailheads may not have facilities.

ACCOMMODATIONS

LODGING INSIDE THE PARK

Staying inside Glacier National Park offers a unique and immersive experience, allowing you to wake up to **towering peaks, pristine lakes, and wildlife right outside your door.** The park features several historic lodges, cozy motor inns, and rustic accommodations that provide both charm and convenience. However, these lodgings fill up **fast**—often a year in advance—so planning ahead is essential. Below is a breakdown of **the best places to stay inside Glacier National Park**, along with tips for securing a reservation and alternative options if lodges are fully booked.

🏨 Many Glacier Hotel – "The Crown Jewel of Glacier"

📍 Location: 1 Many Glacier Road, Babb, MT 59411

⭐ Best For: Iconic Glacier scenery, rustic charm, and access to top hiking trails

Why Stay Here?

- Perched on Swiftcurrent Lake, Many Glacier Hotel offers some of the most breathtaking views in the entire park.

- Built in 1915, this Swiss chalet-style lodge exudes old-world charm with a grand lobby, towering wooden beams, and cozy fireplaces.
- Top-notch wildlife viewing —frequent bear, moose, and bighorn sheep sightings.
- Prime access to Grinnell Glacier, Iceberg Lake, and Swiftcurrent Pass—some of Glacier's best hikes.

Amenities:

- Lakefront rooms with stunning views (but no air conditioning or TVs).
- Ptarmigan Dining Room – Serves breakfast, lunch, and dinner with incredible lake views.
- Horseback riding, boat tours, and guided hikes available nearby.

Booking Tips:

✅ Book at least a year in advance—this is the most sought-after lodge in Glacier.

✅ Request a lake-facing room for the best sunrise and sunset views.

✅ If sold out, check back regularly for cancellations— availability often changes.

📌 Pro Tip: If you can't get a room, at least stop by for a drink in the Swiss Lounge or a meal with a view!

🏨 Lake McDonald Lodge – Historic Charm on the Water

📍 Location: 288 Lake McDonald Ldg Lp, West Glacier, MT 59936

⭐ Best For: Staying on the park's largest lake, easy access to scenic drives and shuttles

Why Stay Here?

- Rustic, historic lodge built in 1913, with a cozy, wood-paneled interior that transports you back in time.
- Stunning lake views with kayak rentals, boat tours, and evening campfires.

Best Room Options:

- Main Lodge Rooms – Cozy, historic rooms (no TVs, AC, or Wi-Fi).
- Cabins & Suites – Offer more space and privacy, great for families.
- Lakefront Cabins – The best choice for a quiet retreat with direct lake access.

Pros & Cons:

✅ Close to Apgar Village, shuttle stops, and many trails.

✅ Great ambiance—the massive stone fireplace in the lobby is a must-see.

❌ Rooms are small & rustic (thin walls, no AC).

❌ High demand—book early!

📌 **Pro Tip:** Even if you don't stay overnight, stop by the lodge's **Russell's Fireside Dining Room** for a meal with lake views.

🏢 Rising Sun Motor Inn – Budget-Friendly, East Side Convenience

📍 Location:Going-to-the-Sun Rd, St Mary, MT 59411,

⭐ Best For: Travelers on a budget who want quick access to St. Mary Lake

Why Stay Here?

- One of the more affordable lodges inside the park, offering simple motel-style rooms and rustic cabins.
- Just 6 miles from Logan Pass, making it one of the best locations for sunrise hikes.

Pros & Cons:

✅ **Cheaper than other lodges** inside Glacier.

✅ **Good location for Going-to-the-Sun Road, boat tours, and hiking.**

❌ **Basic accommodations—** thin walls, no AC, older furnishings.

❌ **Sells out fast due to its affordability.**

Swiftcurrent Motor Inn – A Hiker's Paradise

📍 Location:Glacier National Park, Glacier Dr, Columbia Falls, MT 59912,

⭐ Best For: Hikers looking for an affordable basecamp near Grinnell Glacier & Iceberg Lake

Why Stay Here?

- Most affordable lodging option in Many Glacier.
- Steps from trailheads for some of the park's best hikes.
- More casual and low-key than Many Glacier Hotel, but still within the same stunning valley.

Room Options:

- **Motel Rooms & Cabins –** No-frills but **clean and comfortable.**
- **Some cabins have private bathrooms, others use shared bathhouses.**

Pros & Cons:

✅ Best location for hiking—you can walk right to many trails.

✅ More budget-friendly than Many Glacier Hotel.

❌ No Wi-Fi, no AC, and limited dining options.

📌 Pro Tip: Cabins book up even faster than motel rooms—reserve ASAP!

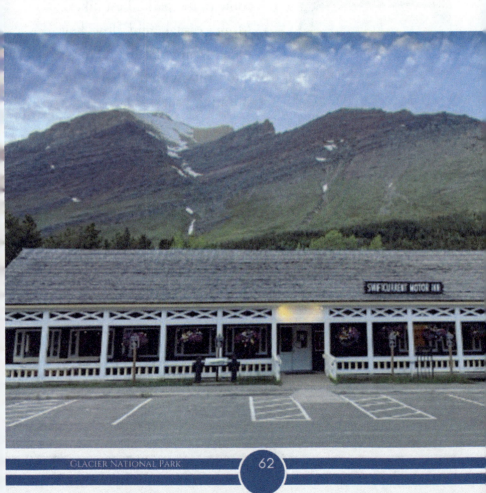

🏨 Village Inn at Apgar – Stunning Lakefront Views

📍 Location: 68 W Apgar Loop Rd, West Glacier, MT 59936

⭐ Best For: Travelers who want a peaceful, lakeside retreat

Why Stay Here?

- Directly on Lake McDonald, with unobstructed water and mountain views.
- Rooms have kitchenettes, great for those who want to cook their own meals.
- Relaxed, family-friendly atmosphere in the heart of Apgar Village.

Pros & Cons:

✅ **Unbeatable sunset views over Lake McDonald.**

✅ **Great for families & longer stays** (some rooms sleep 5-6).

❌ **Sells out fast, especially lake-view rooms.**

❌ **No on-site restaurant,** but eateries are nearby.

📍 **Pro Tip: Book a second-story room** for the best views.

📌 Reservation Tips & Alternatives if Lodges Are Full

How & When to Book

- Reservations open 12-13 months in advance at Glacier National Park Lodges.
- Peak Season (July & August) fills up fast, so book ASAP!
- Check back frequently—cancellations happen!

What to Do If Lodges Are Full?

- Stay in Nearby Towns:
  - West Glacier & Whitefish – Great for exploring Lake McDonald & Going-to-the-Sun Road.
  - St. Mary & Babb – Best for Many Glacier & St. Mary hikes.
- Campgrounds:
  - Many campgrounds, like Apgar and St. Mary, have ADA-accessible sites and amenities.

📍 Pro Tip: Call lodges directly if online reservations are full—sometimes they have last-minute availability!

Camping Sites and Reservations

Camping in **Glacier National Park** is an incredible way to immerse yourself in the park's wild beauty. Whether you're pitching a tent under towering peaks, parking your RV beside a glacier-fed lake, or venturing deep into the backcountry, **there's a camping experience for everyone**. However, **demand is high**, and many campgrounds **fill up months in advance**, so planning ahead is key.

Below, you'll find a breakdown of **the best campgrounds, reservation tips, permit info, RV camping options, and essential safety guidelines** for a smooth and unforgettable camping adventure.

🌲 POPULAR CAMPGROUNDS

1. Apgar Campground – Best for Families & West Side Access

📍 Location: Near Apgar Village, West Glacier

⛺ Size: 194 sites (largest in the park)

📅 Reservations: Available for some sites, others first-come, first-served

🚗 RV-Friendly? ✅ Yes, up to 40 feet

💰 Fee: ~$23 per night

Why Stay Here?

- Close to Lake McDonald, visitor centers, and shuttle stops.
- Has flush toilets, potable water, and picnic tables.
- Great for families and first-time visitors due to easy access.

📌 **Pro Tip:** This is the **largest campground in Glacier**, but it still fills up quickly. **Book early or arrive by 8 AM for first-come sites.**

2. Many Glacier Campground – Best for Hikers & Wildlife Viewing

📍 Location: Many Glacier Valley, Northeast Glacier

⛺ Size: 109 sites

📅 Reservations: Required for summer (mid-June to mid-September)

🚗 RV-Friendly? ✅ Yes, but limited to 35 feet

💰 Fee: ~$23 per night

Why Stay Here?

- Prime access to Grinnell Glacier, Iceberg Lake, and Swiftcurrent Pass trailheads.
- Frequent bear, moose, and mountain goat sightings.
- Flush toilets, potable water, and picnic tables available.

📌 Pro Tip: If you love hiking, this is the best campground in the park—but reservations book up months in advance.

3. St. Mary Campground – Best for East Side & Going-to-the-Sun Road Access

📍 Location: Near St. Mary, East Glacier

🏕️ Size: 148 sites

📅 Reservations: Required

🚗 RV-Friendly? ✅ Yes, up to 40 feet

💰 Fee: ~$23 per night

Why Stay Here?

- Closest campground to the **St. Mary Entrance & Going-to-the-Sun Road.**
- Great for exploring **Logan Pass, St. Mary Lake, and Hidden Lake Overlook.**
- Flush toilets, showers, and potable water available.

📌 Pro Tip: High winds are common in this area—secure your tent well!

🐻 Bear Safety, Food Storage & Weather Tips

🐻 Bear Safety in Glacier

Glacier is bear country, so campers must follow strict food storage rules:

✅ Use bear boxes (provided at most campgrounds).

✅ Carry bear spray (available in West Glacier & St. Mary).

✅ Never leave food or scented items in tents.

🚫 What NOT to do:

❌ Leave food scraps out (even biodegradable waste).

❌ Approach or feed wildlife.

❌ Sleep in clothes worn while cooking.

📌 Pro Tip: Many Glacier and Two Medicine are prime bear habitat—be extra vigilant!

❄️ Weather Considerations

- July-August: Warm days (60-80°F), cool nights (30-50°F).
- September-October: Cold nights (20-40°F), unpredictable snow.
- Heavy winds on the east side—secure your tent well!
- Rain is common—bring waterproof gear.

📌 Pro Tip: If camping at St. Mary or Many Glacier, be prepared for strong winds and cold nights, even in summer!

NEARBY HOTELS AND RENTALS

If lodging inside Glacier National Park is fully booked— or you prefer more amenities—staying just outside the park can be a great option. The surrounding towns of West Glacier, Whitefish, Columbia Falls, and St. Mary offer a variety of accommodations, from budget-friendly motels and rustic cabins to luxury resorts and private vacation rentals.

🏘 Best Hotels & Lodges in West Glacier

📍 Best For: Visitors who want quick park access and a classic Glacier experience.

1. Belton Chalet – Historic Lodge with a Classic Feel

⭐ Best For: Couples, history lovers

💰 Price Range: $$$

📍 Location: Directly outside West Glacier Entrance

✨ Why Stay Here?

- One of Glacier's first railway lodges, built in 1910.
- Elegant yet rustic rooms with a vintage charm (no TVs or AC).
- Fine dining on-site and cozy fire pits for evening relaxation.

📌 Pro Tip: Book early—this lodge fills up fast due to its history and location.

2. Glacier Guides Lodge – Cozy & Quiet Retreat

⭐ Best For: Small groups, outdoor lovers

💰 Price Range: $$

📍 Location: 1 mile from West Glacier Entrance

✨ Why Stay Here?

- Eco-friendly lodge with modern comforts.
- Close to rafting, hiking, and park tours.
- Quiet and peaceful compared to larger lodges.

📌 Pro Tip: This is one of the best-reviewed lodges in West Glacier.

3. Great Northern Resort – Rustic Cabins & Adventure Packages

⭐ **Best For:** Families, adventurers

💰 **Price Range:** $$

📍 **Location:** 2 miles from West Glacier Entrance

✨ **Why Stay Here?**

- **Cozy log cabins with kitchenettes.**
- Offers **whitewater rafting, guided hikes, and fly fishing trips.**

📌 **Pro Tip: Book a package deal** for lodging + guided park tours.

🏨 Best Hotels & Resorts in Whitefish

📍 Best For: Luxury stays, nightlife, and year-round activities.

1. The Lodge at Whitefish Lake – Luxury on the Water

⭐ Best For: Luxury travelers, couples

💰 Price Range: $$$$

📍 Location: 25 miles from Glacier (Whitefish Lake)

✨ Why Stay Here?

- Elegant lodge-style resort with a spa, lakefront dining, and private beach.
- Heated pool, hot tubs, and fireplaces in many rooms.
- Close to Whitefish's lively downtown, full of great restaurants and breweries.

📌 Pro Tip: Stay here for comfort if you don't mind a 45-minute drive to Glacier.

2. Firebrand Hotel – Boutique Luxury in Downtown Whitefish

⭐ Best For: Foodies, nightlife lovers

💰 Price Range: $$$

📍 Location: Whitefish downtown (25 miles from Glacier)

✨ Why Stay Here?

- Trendy, modern hotel with a rooftop hot tub.
- Walkable location near Whitefish's best restaurants and bars.

📌 Pro Tip: Perfect for combining Glacier with a Whitefish weekend getaway.

🏡 Best Lodging in Columbia Falls – Budget-Friendly & Family-Friendly

📍 Best For: Affordable stays and a central location between Glacier and Whitefish.

1. Cedar Creek Lodge – Best Value Hotel Near Glacier

⭐ Best For: Budget-conscious travelers

💰 Price Range: $$

📍 Location: 17 miles from Glacier (Columbia Falls)

✨ Why Stay Here?

- Spacious, modern rooms with AC (a rare Glacier luxury!).
- Free breakfast and indoor pool.
- Great value for families and groups.

📌 Pro Tip: Cheaper than West Glacier hotels but still a short drive to the park.

🏕️ Best Hotels & Lodges in St. Mary – Closest to East Glacier

📍 Best For: Hikers and those exploring Many Glacier & Going-to-the-Sun Road.

1. St. Mary Village – Best for East Glacier Access

⭐ Best For: Convenience, hikers

💰 Price Range: $$-$$$

📍 Location: At St. Mary Entrance

✨ Why Stay Here?

- Multiple lodging options: motel rooms, cabins, and riverside rooms.
- Close to Many Glacier & Going-to-the-Sun Road.
- On-site dining, grocery store, and gift shop.

📌 Pro Tip: The riverside cabins offer the best views!

🏡 **Vacation Rentals, Cabins & Airbnbs**

For a more private and secluded stay, consider vacation rentals or cabins near Glacier.

Luxury Rentals & Cabins ($$$-$$$$)

🏡 Luxury Mountain Lodge (Whitefish) – Private hot tub, 5-star comfort.

🏡 Sky Eco Lodge (Columbia Falls) – Off-grid luxury cabin with panoramic views.

🏡 Montana Treehouse Retreat (Columbia Falls) – Stay in a two-story treehouse!

📌 Pro Tip: Whitefish & Columbia Falls have the best luxury Airbnb options.

Budget-Friendly Rentals ($–$$$)

🏡 **Cozy Cabin Near Glacier (West Glacier)** – Affordable, rustic, sleeps 4.

🏡 **Rising Sun Cabin (St. Mary)** – Perfect for hikers, simple but convenient.

🏡 **Railway Bungalow (Essex, MT)** – Unique lodging near train tracks, great for history buffs.

📌 **Pro Tip: Airbnbs near West Glacier fill up fast!** Book 6+ months in advance.

Insider Tips & Final Recommendations

Choosing where to stay near **Glacier National Park** depends on your interests and the time of year. Here's a quick guide to **the best lodging options based on travel style, alternative stays, and seasonal considerations**.

⛰️ Best Places to Stay by Interest

- 🥾 Hikers: Stay at Many Glacier Hotel or Swiftcurrent Motor Inn for quick trail access to Grinnell Glacier, Iceberg Lake, and Ptarmigan Tunnel.
- 🦌 Wildlife Enthusiasts: St. Mary Lodge and Many Glacier Campground offer prime bear and moose sightings.
- 📷 Photographers: Lake McDonald Lodge for iconic sunrise/sunset reflections or Village Inn at Apgar for panoramic lakefront views.
- 👨‍👩‍👧 Families: Apgar Village Lodge provides easy access to kid-friendly trails, boat rentals, and visitor centers.

TOP ATTRACTIONS

Glacier National Park, often called the "Crown of the Continent," is home to stunning alpine scenery, iconic wildlife, and over 700 miles of hiking trails. Whether you're exploring by car, foot, or boat, here are the must-see attractions you shouldn't miss.

1. Going-to-the-Sun Road

📍 Best For: Scenic drive, photography, wildlife spotting

🚗 Season: Typically open late June to mid-October (dependent on snow conditions)

This 50-mile scenic highway is the most famous attraction in Glacier National Park. Winding through the heart of the park, it offers jaw-dropping views of mountains, waterfalls, and glacial valleys. Must-stop spots include:

- Logan Pass: The highest point on the road at 6,646 feet, often home to mountain goats and bighorn sheep.

- **Wild Goose Island Viewpoint:** A famous photo spot with a tiny island in the middle of St. Mary Lake.
- **The Loop:** A dramatic switchback section with views of the Garden Wall and surrounding peaks.

2. Many Glacier

📍 Best For: Hiking, wildlife viewing, boat tours

🚗 Location: Northeast section of the park

Many Glacier is one of the most scenic areas in the park, known for its towering peaks, glacial lakes, and abundant wildlife. Popular activities include:

- Hiking to Grinnell Glacier: One of the best hikes in the park, featuring turquoise lakes and up-close views of the glacier.
- Swiftcurrent Lake & Josephine Lake Boat Tours: A great way to experience the beauty of the region without a long hike.
- Wildlife Spotting: Look out for moose, bears, and mountain goats.

3. Lake McDonald

📍 Best For: Relaxing, kayaking, photography

🚗 Location: West Glacier, near Apgar Village

Lake McDonald is the largest lake in Glacier National Park, known for its crystal-clear water and multicolored rocks. It's a great spot for:

- Sunset Views: The lake reflects the surrounding peaks, creating a stunning backdrop.
- Boat Rentals & Kayaking: Rent a canoe or kayak from Apgar Village and paddle on the calm waters.
- Hiking to Avalanche Lake: A short, scenic hike leading to a beautiful glacial lake.

4. Logan Pass & Hidden Lake Overlook

Best For: Short hike, panoramic views, wildlife

Trail Length: 2.7 miles round trip to the overlook

Logan Pass is the highest point accessible by car in the park, and it's a prime location for spotting wildlife. The Hidden Lake Overlook trail offers:

- Panoramic views of Hidden Lake and surrounding peaks.
- Chances to see mountain goats, marmots, and occasionally grizzly bears.
- A moderate hike with boardwalks making it accessible to most visitors.

5. Grinnell Glacier

Best For: Hiking, glaciers, photography

Trail Length: 10.6 miles round trip

One of the most famous hikes in the park, the Grinnell Glacier Trail offers:

- Up-close views of an active glacier.
- Stunning alpine scenery, including turquoise lakes and waterfalls.
- Wildlife sightings, such as bears and bighorn sheep.

6. Two Medicine

📍 Best For: Solitude, hiking, scenic boat tours

🚗 Location: Southeast corner of the park

Less crowded than Many Glacier and Going-to-the-Sun Road, Two Medicine offers:

- Boat tours on Two Medicine Lake, leading to shorter hikes to places like Twin Falls.
- Hiking to Scenic Point: A moderate-to-strenuous hike with panoramic views of the Great Plains.
- Waterfall Exploration: Visit Running Eagle Falls, a unique "double waterfall."

7. Bowman Lake & Kintla Lake (North Fork Area)

📍 Best For: Seclusion, camping, paddling

🚗 Location: Remote northwest section of the park

For those seeking solitude, the North Fork area offers:

- Unpaved roads leading to stunning lakes with fewer crowds.
- Great backcountry camping and paddling opportunities.
- A rugged, off-the-beaten-path experience.

8. Avalanche Lake & Trail of the Cedars

📍 **Best For:** Family-friendly hiking, waterfalls, old-growth forests

👢 **Trail Length:** 4.6 miles round trip

This easy hike begins on the Trail of the Cedars, a wheelchair-accessible boardwalk through an ancient cedar forest. It leads to:

- **A stunning glacial lake surrounded by waterfalls.**
- **A peaceful setting with fewer crowds than other lake hikes.**

9. St. Mary Valley & Virginia Falls

📍 **Best For:** Waterfalls, photography, moderate hikes

👢 **Trail Length:** 3.6 miles round trip

The St. Mary Valley, located on the east side of the park, is home to:

- **Virginia Falls:** A stunning multi-tiered waterfall reached by a moderate hike.
- **St. Mary Falls:** A shorter hike to a beautiful turquoise waterfall.
- **Wild Goose Island Overlook:** A must-stop photo opportunity.

OUTDOOR ACTIVITIES

HIKING TRAILS: EASY TO STRENUOUS

Glacier National Park is a hiker's paradise, offering everything from leisurely lakeside strolls to grueling alpine treks that test endurance and reward with jaw-dropping vistas. Whether you're seeking a casual nature walk with the family or an adrenaline-pumping adventure deep in the backcountry, there's a trail for you. Below is a selection of hikes ranging from easy to strenuous, complete with practical details and insider tips to help you make the most of your adventure.

Easy Trails: Scenic Strolls and Family-Friendly Walks

1. Trail of the Cedars

Distance: 1 mile (loop)
Estimated Time: 30 minutes

Elevation Gain: Minimal

Highlights: Ancient western red cedars, wheelchair-accessible boardwalk, Avalanche Creek views

Seasonal Info: Usually accessible from late May through October, depending on snowfall.

Insider Tip: Arrive early in the morning or late afternoon to avoid peak crowds. The boardwalk offers a smooth, accessible path for all ages and abilities.

This gentle, shaded trail immerses you in a lush forest of towering cedars and hemlocks, a rare sight in the park. The sound of Avalanche Creek cascading through the narrow gorge creates a tranquil atmosphere, and the occasional burst of sunlight filtering through the dense canopy adds a magical touch.

2. Hidden Lake Overlook

Distance: 2.8 miles (round trip)

Estimated Time: 1.5–2 hours

Elevation Gain: 540 feet

Highlights: Panoramic views of Hidden Lake, wildflower meadows, mountain goats

Seasonal Info: Usually accessible from July to early October due to lingering snow.

Insider Tip: Bring binoculars for wildlife spotting—mountain goats frequently lounge near the overlook. Snowfields often persist into summer, so wear appropriate footwear.

Moderate Trails: Immersive Adventures with Stunning Views

3. Avalanche Lake

Distance: 4.6 miles (round trip)

Estimated Time: 2–3 hours

Elevation Gain: 730 feet

Highlights: Avalanche Creek, emerald lake, waterfalls cascading from cliffs

Seasonal Info: Best from late May through October; snow may linger in early spring.

Insider Tip: Arrive early in summer to secure parking at the Trail of the Cedars lot. Mosquitoes can be aggressive near the lake—bring insect repellent!

This hike begins along the Trail of the Cedars and follows Avalanche Creek upstream through a narrow gorge. As you climb, the sound of rushing water fades, replaced by the quiet rustle of towering firs and pines. The grand reveal—Avalanche Lake, ringed by sheer cliffs with waterfalls tumbling from unseen glaciers above—is a sight worth every step.

4. Highline Trail (to Haystack Pass)

Distance: 7.2 miles (round trip)

Estimated Time: 3–5 hours

Elevation Gain: 1,150 feet

Highlights: Jaw-dropping vistas, wildflowers, possible grizzly sightings

Seasonal Info: Typically open from early July to October; snow can persist on exposed sections.

Insider Tip: Those afraid of heights should be cautious —the trail has a narrow, cliffside section with a hand cable.

Starting at Logan Pass, this trail hugs the edge of the Continental Divide, offering uninterrupted views of glacially sculpted valleys and distant peaks. The first few miles are particularly scenic, with lush meadows and rocky ledges teeming with marmots, bighorn sheep, and the occasional grizzly bear sighting. Haystack Pass makes for a fantastic turnaround point if you're not up for the full 11.8-mile trek to Granite Park Chalet.

Planning Your Glacier National Park Hike

- **Permits & Fees:** Some trails, like Grinnell Glacier, require a day-use permit in peak season. Backcountry routes require overnight camping permits.
- **Wildlife Awareness:** Glacier is bear country—carry bear spray and make noise while hiking.
- **Trail Conditions:** Snow and ice linger on higher-elevation trails well into summer. Check current conditions before heading out.
- **Weather Prep:** Afternoon thunderstorms are common—start early and bring rain gear.
- **Leave No Trace:** Pack out all trash and respect the fragile alpine ecosystem.

WILDLIFE VIEWING SPOTS

Glacier National Park is a haven for wildlife enthusiasts, offering some of the best chances in the Lower 48 to spot iconic species like grizzly bears, mountain goats, bighorn sheep, and moose. The park's diverse terrain—from alpine meadows to dense forests—creates a perfect habitat for these creatures. Here's where to go and how to make the most of your wildlife viewing experience.

Top Wildlife Viewing Areas

1. Many Glacier Valley

Often called the "Serengeti of North America," Many Glacier is prime territory for grizzlies, moose, and bighorn sheep. Early mornings and late evenings are the best times to see bears foraging near Swiftcurrent Lake and Fishercap Lake. Moose frequent the shallows, especially in the quieter hours.

2. Logan Pass (Going-to-the-Sun Road)

This high-altitude pass is one of the best spots to see mountain goats and bighorn sheep up close. The Hidden Lake Overlook Trail often has goats grazing near the trail, completely unfazed by human presence. Bighorn sheep can be spotted on rocky slopes near the visitor center.

3. Two Medicine

Less crowded than Many Glacier, Two Medicine offers excellent moose sightings, especially near Pray Lake and along the South Shore Trail. Keep an eye out for black bears in the dense forests.

4. North Fork & Bowman Lake

This remote area sees fewer visitors, making it a peaceful place to encounter elk, wolves, and even the elusive lynx. Drive the Camas Road at dawn or dusk for a chance to see wildlife along the tree line.

5. Goat Lick Overlook

True to its name, this roadside pullout near Essex is a hotspot for mountain goats. They gather here to lick the mineral-rich cliffs, providing a rare, easy-to-access viewing opportunity.

Best Times for Sightings

- **Early Morning (Dawn) & Late Evening (Dusk):** Wildlife is most active when temperatures are cooler and human activity is low.
- **Spring (May–June):** Bears emerge from hibernation, and newborn animals make their first appearances.
- **Fall (September–October):** Elk and moose are in rut, and bears are hyperphagic (preparing for hibernation), making them more visible.

Wildlife Viewing Tips

- **Stay Safe:** Maintain a **minimum of 100 yards** from bears and wolves, 25 yards from all other wildlife. Use binoculars or a zoom lens for close-up views.
- **Be Quiet & Patient:** Move slowly, avoid loud noises, and let the wildlife come to you.
- **Carry Bear Spray:** Essential for safety, especially in grizzly territory. Know how to use it before hitting the trail.
- **Follow Park Guidelines:** Never feed wildlife, and always store food properly to avoid attracting animals to campsites.

Scenic Drives & Trails for Wildlife Watching

- **Going-to-the-Sun Road:** Incredible wildlife spotting along its entire length, especially around Logan Pass and Big Bend.
- **Iceberg Lake Trail:** Bears are frequently seen along this trail, so hike with caution.
- **Avalanche Lake Trail:** Great for spotting deer, smaller mammals, and the occasional black bear.
- **Highline Trail:** Known for mountain goats and breathtaking scenery.

Glacier National Park's wildlife is part of what makes this place magical. Whether you're watching a grizzly from a safe distance or spotting a moose in a misty morning lake, these encounters will stay with you long after you leave. Respect the animals, stay safe, and enjoy one of the most spectacular wildlife experiences in the world.

Boating and Fishing Opportunities

Glacier National Park is a paradise for water enthusiasts, with its glacially carved lakes, swift-flowing rivers, and serene backcountry waters offering a range of boating and fishing opportunities. Whether you're paddling across a mirror-like alpine lake, testing your skills in a cold, rushing river, or casting your line for native trout, the park's waterways provide an unforgettable experience.

Best Lakes and Rivers for Boating

Canoeing, Kayaking, and Paddleboarding

For those seeking a peaceful paddle amid stunning mountain scenery, Glacier's lakes deliver in every season. **Lake McDonald**, the park's largest lake, is a favorite for early-morning kayakers and paddle boarders who want to glide over its calm, crystal-clear waters while taking in views of towering peaks.

The far end of the lake, near the **Apgar Village**, is ideal for launching, and rentals are available at Apgar and Lake McDonald Lodge.

For a more secluded experience, **Bowman Lake** in the park's remote North Fork region is a paddler's dream. The drive to the lake is rugged, but the reward is solitude, pristine waters, and a backdrop of the Livingston Range. **Kintla Lake**, even farther north, offers an even greater sense of wilderness, but no rentals are available, so bring your own canoe or kayak.

Motorized Boating

Motorboats are permitted on select lakes, including **Lake McDonald, St. Mary Lake, Two Medicine Lake, and Waterton Lake**. These vast waters provide excellent opportunities for leisurely cruising, photography, and fishing. Boat rentals and guided tours are available at Lake McDonald and St. Mary Lake, allowing visitors to explore without the hassle of bringing their own vessel.

River Adventures

The **Flathead River System**—comprising the North, Middle, and South Forks—forms the park's western boundary and offers thrilling opportunities for rafting and kayaking. The Middle Fork, in particular, is renowned for its mix of calm stretches and exhilarating rapids.

Top Fishing Spots & Regulations

Glacier's cold, clean waters are home to several species of trout and other native fish. Anglers will find a mix of fly-fishing, spin fishing, and traditional angling opportunities throughout the park.

- **Lake McDonald:** While fish populations are lower here due to the lake's depth, persistent anglers may hook **bull trout** (catch-and-release only) or **lake trout**.

- **St. Mary Lake:** This glacial-fed lake holds **cutthroat trout, rainbow trout, and whitefish**. Fly-fishing along the shore or trolling from a boat can be productive.

- **Many Glacier Lakes (Swiftcurrent, Josephine, and Sherburne Lakes):** These lakes are known for **cutthroat trout** and the occasional brook trout. The shorelines offer excellent wading spots for fly-fishers.

- **North Fork and Middle Fork of the Flathead River:** These Wild and Scenic rivers are among the best fly-fishing waters in Montana. Expect to catch **native cutthroat trout** and **whitefish** in these pristine waters.

Regulations & Permits:

- No state fishing license is required for fishing within the park, but **special regulations apply** to protect native fish populations.
- **Catch-and-release is mandatory** for bull trout.
- **Artificial lures and single, barbless hooks** are required in many areas to minimize harm to fish.
- **Seasons vary**: Some lakes and rivers are open year-round, while others close seasonally to protect spawning fish. Check with park rangers for current rules before casting your line.

Boat Rentals, Guided Fishing Trips & Safety Tips

- **Boat Rentals:** Visitors can rent canoes, kayaks, and small motor boats at **Lake McDonald Lodge** and **Two Medicine Lake**.
- **Guided Fishing Trips:** Local outfitters in **West Glacier, St. Mary, and Babb** offer half-day and full-day guided fishing excursions, both from shore and by boat.
- **Bear Awareness:** Always carry bear spray and make noise when fishing or launching from remote shorelines.
- **Cold Water Caution:** Glacier's waters remain **frigid even in summer**. Wear a life jacket at all times and be prepared for sudden weather changes.
- **Aquatic Invasive Species Check:** All boats, including kayaks and paddleboards, **must undergo inspection** before entering park waters.

GUIDED TOURS AND RANGER PROGRAMS

A visit to Glacier National Park isn't complete without diving deeper into its rich landscapes, history, and wildlife through its guided tours and ranger-led programs. Whether you're eager to explore the park's iconic trails with an expert naturalist, cruise the pristine glacial lakes, or immerse yourself in the cultural heritage of the Blackfeet Nation, there's an experience waiting for you.

Ranger-Led Hikes and Programs

Glacier National Park offers a variety of **ranger-led hikes**, **educational talks**, and **evening campfire programs** designed to enhance your understanding of the park's ecosystems, geology, and wildlife. These free programs, offered throughout the summer season, provide a deeper connection to the park's wonders.

- **Guided Day Hikes**: Join a park ranger for an insightful trek along some of Glacier's most scenic trails. Popular options include hikes to Avalanche Lake, Hidden Lake Overlook, and St. Mary Falls, where rangers share fascinating insights into glacial formations, flora, and fauna. Difficulty levels range from easy walks to more strenuous excursions.

- **Evening Campfire Programs:** Unwind at the amphitheaters of popular campgrounds like Apgar, Many Glacier, and Rising Sun, where rangers host engaging storytelling sessions on the park's history, wildlife behavior, and conservation efforts.
- **Wildlife and Geology Talks:** Held at visitor centers and scenic pullouts, these talks provide a fascinating look at Glacier's unique landscapes, from its towering peaks to the ever-shrinking glaciers that define the park.

How to Join: No reservations required. Simply check the daily schedule at a visitor center or online via the National Park Service website. Programs run from late June through mid-September.

Red Bus Tours: A Ride Through Time

One of the most iconic ways to experience Glacier is aboard the historic **Red Bus Tours.** These vintage 1930s buses, with their open-air tops, allow passengers to take in breathtaking 360-degree views while learning about the park's history, wildlife, and geology from expert guides. Tours range from **half-day trips to full-day excursions** and traverse legendary routes like Going-to-the-Sun Road, Many Glacier, and Two Medicine.

Insider Tip: The best seats are in the back row for unobstructed panoramic views. Early summer tours may be subject to weather delays due to snowpack on the road.

Booking & Costs: Reservations are highly recommended and can be made through **Glacier National Park Lodges**. Prices range from **$50 to $120 per person**, depending on the route.

Boat Cruises on Glacier's Pristine Lakes

For a tranquil yet awe-inspiring experience, hop aboard a **scenic boat tour** operated by Glacier Park Boat Company. These historic wooden boats glide across the park's glacially-carved lakes, offering unmatched perspectives on towering cliffs, cascading waterfalls, and potential wildlife sightings.

- **Lake McDonald Cruise:** A leisurely ride on the park's largest lake, with reflections of forested peaks in the crystal-clear waters.
- **Two Medicine Lake:** A hidden gem with stunning mountain backdrops and the option to combine your cruise with a guided hike.
- **Swiftcurrent Lake and Josephine Lake (Many Glacier):** The perfect excursion for spotting moose and grizzlies along the shore.
- **St. Mary Lake:** Home to the famous Wild Goose Island and surrounded by dramatic mountain scenery.

Booking & Costs: Advance reservations are recommended, particularly in July and August. Cruises cost between **$18 and $40 per adult**, with discounts for children.

Cultural Programs with the Blackfeet Nation

Glacier National Park is deeply intertwined with the history and traditions of the **Blackfeet Nation**, whose ancestral lands include much of the park. Visitors can partake in **Blackfeet cultural tours**, storytelling sessions, and educational events to gain a deeper appreciation for the Indigenous history of the region.

- **Sun Tours:** Led by Blackfeet guides, these unique bus tours offer a perspective on Glacier's landscapes through the lens of Native traditions, folklore, and spirituality.
- **Cultural Demonstrations:** At St. Mary Visitor Center, Blackfeet artisans and storytellers share traditional music, crafts, and historical accounts of their deep connection to the land.
- **Tipi Encampment Experiences:** Near East Glacier, visitors can immerse themselves in a hands-on experience learning about Blackfeet customs and traditions.

Booking & Costs: Sun Tours can be booked online or at St. Mary Visitor Center, with rates starting around **$65 per adult.**

Planning Tips for Your Guided Experience

- **Book in Advance**: Red Bus Tours, boat cruises, and Sun Tours fill up quickly—reserve as early as possible.
- **Check the Weather**: Glacier's conditions change rapidly, and certain tours may be delayed or canceled due to weather.
- **Dress in Layers**: Even in summer, temperatures can drop significantly in the mountains.
- **Arrive Early**: Many ranger programs and tours depart from popular locations that can get crowded —plan to arrive at least 30 minutes before departure.
- **Ask Questions**: Rangers and guides are an incredible resource—don't hesitate to engage with them to enhance your experience.

ADVENTURE ITINERARIES

ONE-DAY HIGHLIGHTS

Route & Timing:

- Start Early: Begin around 6:30–7:00 AM from the West Glacier area (near Apgar Village or Lake McDonald). Early hours offer dramatic sunrise views over Lake McDonald and help beat the summer crowds.

- Drive the Iconic Route: Cruise along Going-to-the-Sun Road. Enjoy the shifting landscapes—from the mirror-like surface of Lake McDonald to the rugged alpine vistas. Photo stops along the way (e.g., near Wild Goose Island) are highly recommended.

- Key Landmark: Aim to reach Logan Pass by about 9:30–10:00 AM. At this high-altitude point, you'll be greeted by sweeping views and interpretive exhibits at the Visitor Center.

Practical Tips:

- Parking: Logan Pass has limited parking; arriving early is crucial to secure a spot.
- Weather Considerations: Mornings can be chilly, even in summer—bring layered clothing and sun protection.
- Fuel & Supplies: Fill up before entering the park; service is limited inside. Pack water, snacks, and a map (cell service is sporadic).

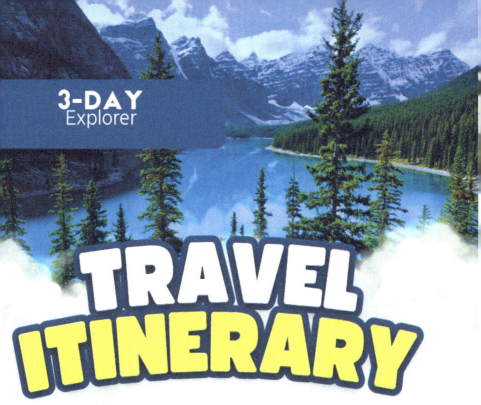

TRAVEL ITINERARY

Day 1: Essential Highlights & Popular Attractions

Morning – Iconic Scenic Drive

- Route & Timing:
  - Start Early (6:30–7:00 AM): Depart from the West Glacier area (Apgar Village or Lake McDonald).
  - Drive Going-to-the-Sun Road: Enjoy early morning light along the route with stops at scenic pullouts such as the overlook near Wild Goose Island.
  - Key Stop: Arrive at Logan Pass around 9:30–10:00 AM for panoramic vistas and a visit to the Visitor Center.

- **Meal Suggestion:**
  - Pack a light breakfast or grab a coffee on the go, as food options along the road are limited.
- **Practical Tips:**
  - Arrive early at Logan Pass to secure parking.
  - Bring layered clothing, as temperatures can vary.
  - Carry water, snacks, and a detailed park map.

Midday – Classic Hike at Logan Pass

- **Hike:**
  - **Hidden Lake Overlook Trail:** A 2–3-mile round-trip offering wildflower meadows, glacier-carved valley views, and photo opportunities.
  - **Timing:** Start around 10:00–10:30 AM to complete the hike by early afternoon.
- **Meal:**
  - Enjoy a picnic lunch on the trail or at a designated rest area near Logan Pass.

Afternoon – St. Mary Lake & Visitor Center

- Route:
  - Drive east along Going-to-the-Sun Road (approximately 45–60 minutes) to the St. Mary area.

- **Stop:** Relax at St. Mary Lake around 1:00–2:00 PM and visit the St. Mary Visitor Center for insights into the region's natural history.
- **Evening:**
  - **Dinner & Lodging Options:**
    - Consider dining at a lodge restaurant (e.g., Lake McDonald Lodge or Many Glacier Hotel) or plan a picnic dinner if you're staying in a more remote campground.
    - Book accommodations well in advance as in-park lodging fills up quickly.
- **Safety:**
  - Monitor weather updates, as mountain conditions can change rapidly.
  - Stay alert for wildlife on the roads.

DAY 2: OUTDOOR ADVENTURES – HIKING, WILDLIFE, & GUIDED TOURS

Morning – Wildlife Viewing in Many Glacier
- **Route & Timing:**
  - **Early Start (around 6:00–7:00 AM):** Head toward the Many Glacier area (roughly a 1-hour drive from your base in the central park).
  - Wildlife Spotting: Early hours are ideal for sightings of moose, bears, and bighorn sheep near Swiftcurrent Lake.

- **Guided Option:**
  - Consider joining a guided wildlife tour or hike, which can offer expert insights on lesser-known trails and local fauna.
- **Meal:**
  - Have a hearty breakfast at your lodge or pack one to eat en route.

Midday – Adventure on the Trails
- **Hiking Options:**
  - **Grinnell Glacier Trail (Partial):** For those seeking a challenge, tackle a portion of this iconic (and strenuous) route.
  - **Alternatives:** If you prefer a moderate pace, explore trails like Ptarmigan Tunnel (seasonal) or a guided hike that delves into the park's hidden trails.
- **Meal:**
  - Enjoy a packed lunch or stop at a local café (if available) near the Many Glacier area.

Afternoon – Exploring Lesser-Known Paths
- **Activities:**
  - Continue on a guided tour or self-led hike through off-the-beaten-path trails, such as the Big Tree Trail or the Red Rock Canyon Trail.
  - Stop by the Many Glacier Hotel area for an afternoon tea or snack break while soaking in the serene lakeside views.

- **Evening:**
  - **Return & Dinner:** Head back to your lodge and dine at the in-house restaurant or a nearby eatery.
  - **Lodging:** Options include the Many Glacier Hotel or nearby cabins/campgrounds. Reservations are essential.
- **Safety:**
  - Carry bear spray and stay informed of current trail conditions.
  - Ensure you have sufficient water, layered clothing, and emergency supplies.

DAY 3: CULTURAL, HISTORICAL & OFF-THE-BEATEN-PATH EXPERIENCES

Morning – Exploring Historic & Remote Areas

- **Route & Timing:**
  - **Start (7:00–8:00 AM):** Begin with a scenic drive along Many Glacier Road, venturing into more remote parts of the park.
  - **Historic Stop:** Visit Apgar Lookout or nearby historic structures around Lake McDonald to glimpse early park history.
  - Meal:
  - Enjoy breakfast at a local diner or your lodge before setting out.

Midday – Two Medicine & Native Heritage
- **Destination:**
  - **Two Medicine Area:** Known for its quieter atmosphere and rich Native American history, explore this less crowded region.
  - **Hiking:** Consider a short trail like Running Eagle Falls or another scenic loop around Two Medicine Lake.
- **Meal:**
  - Pack a picnic lunch to enjoy near the lake, or sample local flavors at a nearby café if available.

Afternoon – Cultural Exploration & Reflection
- **Activities:**
  - Visit a cultural center or check for any ranger-led programs highlighting the traditions of the Blackfeet Nation and early explorers.
  - Alternatively, explore historic chalets or interpretive exhibits that offer insight into the park's past.

Evening:
- **Return & Dinner:** Conclude your day with a relaxed drive back to your base.
- **Lodging Options:** Either return to your previous accommodation (e.g., Many Glacier or West Glacier) or choose a local lodge in the Two Medicine area to experience a quieter end to your trip.

- **Safety & Seasonal Advice:**
    - Check for seasonal road closures or limited services in more remote areas.
    - Ensure you have up-to-date weather information and adequate supplies as amenities may be sparse off the main routes.

Final Tips for Maximizing Your Trip
- **Plan & Reserve:**
    - Book lodging, guided tours, and any special activities well in advance, especially during peak season.
- **Food & Supplies:**
    - Bring ample water, snacks, and layered clothing to handle the variable mountain weather.
    - Carry a detailed map, as cell service is limited in many areas.
- **Flexible Pacing:**
    - While the itinerary is structured, allow time for spontaneous stops or detours. Some of the best experiences in Glacier are found off the beaten path.
- **Respect the Environment:**
    - Follow Leave No Trace principles, maintain a safe distance from wildlife, and respect cultural sites.

WEEK-LONG IMMERSION

Day 1: Arrival & Orientation

- **Morning:**
  - **Arrive & Check-In:** Settle into your chosen base (e.g., West Glacier, Lake McDonald Lodge, or Many Glacier Hotel).
  - **Visitor Center Stop:** Pick up maps, current road conditions, and schedule information.
- **Afternoon:**
  - **Light Exploration:** Take a gentle walk around your lodging area (e.g., along Lake McDonald or a nearby trail).
  - **Local Interaction:** Chat with park rangers or local staff to get insider tips.
- **Evening:**
  - **Dinner:** Enjoy a meal at your lodge or a local eatery.
  - **Alternative (Bad Weather):** Visit an indoor visitor center or local museum to learn about the park's natural and cultural history.

Day 4: Off-the-Beaten-Path Gems & Local Guided Tours

- **Morning:**
  - **Explore Two Medicine:** Drive to the Two Medicine area—less crowded yet rich in history and natural beauty.
  - **Hike:** Consider a moderate trail like Running Eagle Falls or a short loop around Two Medicine Lake.
- **Midday:**
  - **Guided Cultural Tour:** Check for ranger-led interpretive programs or local Native American cultural tours that provide context on the Blackfeet Nation's heritage.
  - **Meal:** Enjoy a picnic lunch by the lake or stop at a local café if available.
- **Afternoon:**
  - **Scenic Relaxation:** Explore an off-the-beaten-path viewpoint or a quiet trail to absorb the tranquility of the area.
- **Alternative:**
  - If trails are damp or unsafe, switch to a visit to the Two Medicine Visitor Center or indoor cultural exhibits.

Day 5: Cultural & Historical Exploration

- **Morning:**
  - **Historical Sites:** Visit landmarks such as Apgar Lookout near Lake McDonald and historic structures that reveal the early exploration of the park.
  - **Local Interaction:** Engage with interpretive displays at visitor centers detailing the park's history and the indigenous heritage.
- **Midday:**
  - **Meal:** Dine at a local diner or your lodge's restaurant—sampling regional cuisine adds to the cultural immersion.
  - **Self-Guided Tour:** Use brochures available at visitor centers for a self-guided historical tour.
- **Afternoon:**
  - **Cultural Programs:** Attend any available ranger-led sessions or local presentations about the park's history.
  - **Alternative:**
    - If outdoor conditions aren't favorable, spend extra time at indoor exhibits or check local schedules for film screenings and talks.

Day 6: Extended Adventure & Wildlife Encounters

- **Morning:**
  - **Long Hike:** Tackle a longer trail such as the Highline Trail (from Logan Pass) or another challenging route suited to your fitness level.
  - **Start Early:** Begin before 7:00 AM to maximize daylight and minimize crowds.
- **Midday:**
  - **On-Trail Meal:** Carry an energy-rich lunch, plenty of water, and snacks. Use rest stops to enjoy the panoramic vistas.
- **Afternoon:**
  - **Wildlife Focus:** Continue the hike with extra attention to spotting local fauna.
  - **Return:** Head back in the late afternoon, and enjoy a relaxing evening at your lodge.
- **Gear:**
  - Ensure you have a hydration pack, proper navigation aids, sun and rain protection, and bear safety measures.
- **Alternative:**
  - If weather worsens, shorten your planned hike or shift to a scenic drive with indoor wildlife education sessions available at nearby visitor centers.

Day 7: Relaxation, Reflection & Local Community Interaction

- **Morning:**
    - **Leisurely Start:** Enjoy a relaxed breakfast and a gentle walk near your accommodation.
    - **Favorite Spot:** Revisit a favored viewpoint or lakeside (such as St. Mary or Lake McDonald) for one last moment of reflection.
- **Midday:**
    - **Local Town Visit:** Head to a nearby community like Whitefish or Browning. Explore local galleries, shops, and cafes to experience the regional culture.
    - **Meal:** Savor a locally sourced lunch while interacting with residents and hearing local stories.
- **Afternoon:**
    - **Final Scenic Drive:** Take one last drive along a less-traveled park road or revisit an overlooked trail.
    - **Pack Up & Reflect:** Use the quiet moments to capture final photos and memories.
- **Alternative:**
    - In poor weather, spend additional time in local museums, indoor cafes, or catch a community event if available.

Practical Considerations Throughout the Week

- **Transportation:**
  - A rental car is essential. Monitor daily conditions for key routes like Going-to-the-Sun Road; plan alternative routes if needed.
- **Meal Planning:**
  - Mix packed picnics with meals at lodges and local eateries. A cooler stocked with essentials is advised.
- **Lodging:**
  - Book in-park accommodations (Many Glacier Hotel, Lake McDonald Lodge) or nearby towns (West Glacier, Whitefish) well in advance.
- **Necessary Gear:**
  - Sturdy hiking boots, layered clothing, rain gear, sun protection, insect repellent, bear spray, detailed maps, and a GPS device (cell service is limited).
- **Guided Tours & Local Interaction:**
  - Check park schedules for ranger-led hikes, cultural presentations, and wildlife tours. Local tour operators can provide enriching off-the-beaten-path experiences.
- **Weather & Unexpected Closures:**
  - Stay updated via the official Glacier National Park website or visitor centers. Adapt by opting for indoor attractions, shorter walks, or local cultural activities when necessary.

FLORA AND FAUNA

COMMON WILDLIFE SPECIES

Glacier National Park is a vast and untamed wilderness, where jagged peaks and alpine meadows shelter some of North America's most iconic wildlife. From the formidable grizzly bear to the elusive wolverine, the park teems with life, offering visitors a chance to witness animals in their natural habitats—if they know where (and when) to look.

The Heavyweights: Grizzly and Black Bears

Grizzly bears (Ursus arctos horribilis) reign as the park's apex predator, their massive humps and silver-tipped fur making them unmistakable. Unlike black bears (Ursus americanus), which have a more varied coat color (ranging from cinnamon to jet black) and lack the prominent shoulder hump, grizzlies tend to frequent open meadows and high-country terrain.

Where to See Them:

- **Many Glacier and Two Medicine** are prime grizzly territory, particularly in spring when bears emerge from hibernation, ravenous for roots, berries, and the occasional carrion.
- **Logan Pass** and the **Highline Trail** are also known for bear sightings, especially in late summer when the subalpine meadows burst with huckleberries.

Safety Tip: Always carry bear spray, travel in groups, and make noise on the trail to avoid surprise encounters. If you see a bear, maintain at least **100 yards** of distance and never run—back away slowly instead.

The Mountain Monarchs: Goats and Bighorn Sheep

No trip to Glacier is complete without spotting a **mountain goat** (*Oreamnos americanus*), the park's unofficial mascot. These nimble climbers perch on sheer rock faces, their shaggy white coats blending into the cliffs. Bighorn sheep (*Ovis canadensis*), with their iconic curved horns, roam the park's rugged ridges, often in bachelor groups or protective herds.

Where to See Them:

- **Logan Pass** is the best place to watch mountain goats up close, especially near the Hidden Lake Overlook.
- **The Goat Lick Overlook** along U.S. Highway 2 offers a fascinating spectacle—goats descending to mineral-rich cliffs to lick essential salts.
- Bighorn sheep are frequently seen along **Many Glacier Road** and **Siyeh Bend**.

The Gentle Giants: Moose and Elk

Despite their towering size, **moose** (*Alces alces*) are elusive creatures, often seen wading through marshy areas at dawn or dusk. With their long legs and bulbous snouts, they are built for deep snow and dense thickets. **Elk** (*Cervus canadensis*), by contrast, are social and easier to spot, especially in fall when bugling bulls vie for dominance.

Where to See Them:

- Moose frequent **Fishercap Lake** near Many Glacier and **the wetlands around St. Mary Lake**.
- Elk herds are most active in **the North Fork region** and **Two Medicine Valley**, particularly during the autumn rut.

The Elusive Predators: Wolverines and Lynx

Few visitors are lucky enough to glimpse **wolverines** (*Gulo gulo*) or **Canada lynx** (*Lynx canadensis*), two of Glacier's rarest and most secretive residents. Wolverines, known for their relentless endurance, roam vast distances, while lynx, with their tufted ears and snowshoe-like paws, stealthily hunt snowshoe hares in the dense forests.

Where to See Them:

- Both species prefer remote, high-elevation forests. The **Belly River Valley** and **Gunsight Pass** offer the best—though still rare—opportunities for sightings.
- Winter trekking tours occasionally yield wolverine evidence, like their distinctive five-toed prints.

Feathered Icons: Eagles, Falcons, and Ducks

Glacier's skies are patrolled by bald eagles (Haliaeetus leucocephalus), regal hunters that often scan the lakes for fish. Peregrine falcons (Falco peregrinus), the fastest birds in the world, nest on towering cliffs, while harlequin ducks (Histrionicus histrionicus) brave Glacier's icy streams with striking plumage.

Where to See Them:

- Bald eagles often soar over Lake McDonald and St. Mary Lake, particularly in early morning.
- Peregrine falcons favor the cliffs of Many Glacier and the St. Mary area.
- Harlequin ducks bob through McDonald Creek, their vibrant colors contrasting with the rushing water.

Unlikely Survivors: Reptiles and Amphibians

Despite its harsh winters, Glacier is home to resilient cold-blooded creatures. The **boreal chorus frog** (*Pseudacris maculata*) can survive being nearly frozen solid, while the **western terrestrial garter snake** (*Thamnophis elegans*) emerges on sunny slopes, often near lakeshores.

Where to See Them:

- Look for boreal chorus frogs near **lower elevation wetlands and ponds,** especially in spring when their calls fill the air.

- Garter snakes are most often seen sunning themselves along **McDonald Creek** and **the park's riverbanks.**

Ethical Wildlife Viewing: How to Observe Without Disturbing

- **Keep Your Distance**: Always stay at least **100 yards from bears and wolves** and **25 yards from other wildlife**.
- **Use Binoculars**: A good pair of binoculars or a spotting scope lets you observe animals up close without intruding.
- **Stay on Trails**: Straying off-trail can damage fragile habitat and disrupt animal movement.
- **Do Not Feed Wildlife**: Human food habituation leads to dangerous animal behavior. Keep a clean camp and pack out all waste.
- **Respect the Seasons**: Spring and summer are the best times to see bears and ungulates, while winter offers a glimpse into the secretive lives of lynx and wolverines.

NOTABLE PLANT LIFE

Glacier National Park isn't just about mountains and glaciers—it's also a place where forests, meadows, and alpine slopes create a rich, ever-changing landscape of plant life. Some plants, like western red cedars, have stood for centuries in the deep valleys, while others, like beargrass, make rare and spectacular appearances when conditions are just right. As the seasons shift, so does the park's color palette—wildflowers in summer, golden larch trees in fall, and deep green evergreens standing firm through winter.

From Lush Forests to High Alpine Slopes

As you move through the park, the plant life changes with elevation, moisture, and exposure to wind and snow.

- **Lower Elevations (3,500–5,000 feet)** – The valleys, especially on the wetter west side, are home to thick forests of western red cedar, hemlock, and Douglas fir. On the drier east side, lodgepole pine and aspen are more common.

- Mid-Elevation (5,000–7,000 feet) – Subalpine fir and whitebark pine grow near the tree line, where winters are long and snow lingers well into summer. Open meadows burst into bloom as soon as the snow melts.

- Alpine Zone (Above 7,000 feet) – Harsh winds, cold temperatures, and short growing seasons make it tough for anything to survive. Tiny wildflowers, mosses, and lichens cling to rocky outcrops, adding splashes of color to the otherwise stark landscape.

Plants That Define Glacier National Park

Beargrass

Beargrass is one of the most photographed plants in the park, and for good reason. In early summer, its tall white flowers rise above the greenery, glowing in the sunlight. But here's the catch—it doesn't bloom every year. Some plants wait five to seven years before flowering, which makes catching a full bloom all the more special.

Best Places to See It:
- Highline Trail and Logan Pass (July)
- Two Medicine and Many Glacier (Early summer)

Glacier Lilies

- These bright yellow flowers are among the first to appear when the snow melts, often growing in large clusters. Bears and other animals rely on them for food in early spring, making them an important part of the park's ecosystem.
- **Where to Find Them:**
- **Hidden Lake Overlook** (Late June)
- **Iceberg Lake Trail** (Early summer)

Western Red Cedar

Some of the biggest trees in the park are western red cedars. They grow in Glacier's old-growth forests, reaching heights of over **100 feet** and living for **500 years or more**. Their thick, reddish bark peels in strips, and their branches droop gracefully, creating a peaceful, almost prehistoric feel.

Best Places to Walk Among Them:
- **Trail of the Cedars**
- **Avalanche Lake Trail**

Whitebark Pine

Whitebark pines are survivors. They grow in high, exposed areas where most trees can't. Their seeds provide a crucial food source for wildlife, including grizzly bears. These trees are disappearing due to disease and climate change, but you can still find them clinging to ridgelines across the park.

Where to Spot Them:
- **Logan Pass and Siyeh Pass**
- **Swiftcurrent Pass**

Subalpine Fir

With its narrow, pointed shape, subalpine fir is built for heavy snow. It grows at higher elevations, mixed in with spruce and other conifers. The soft needles have a bluish tint, and its cones sit upright along the branches like little candles.

Best Places to See It:

- **Highline Trail**
- **Two Medicine Valley**

Seasons of Change

Glacier's plant life doesn't stay the same year-round. Each season brings something new.

Spring (May–June): The First Signs of Life

As the snow melts, the valleys turn green, and wildflowers start popping up. Glacier lilies are among the first to bloom, often seen in large clusters near melting snowfields.

Summer (July–August): Peak Bloom

This is when the park is at its most colorful. Beargrass, paintbrush, fireweed, and asters cover meadows, while forests are full and lush.

Best Wildflower Spots:

- **Logan Pass** (July)
- **Iceberg Lake and Grinnell Glacier Trails** (Mid-to-late summer)

Fall (September–October): Golden Larch Season

Western larch is one of the few conifers that loses its needles in fall, but before they drop, they turn bright gold. Entire mountainsides glow with color, making autumn one of the best times to visit.

Best Places to See Larches:

- **North Fork and Bowman Lake**
- **Two Medicine and Lake McDonald Valleys**

Winter (November–April): A Silent Landscape

Snow covers most of the park, and plant life goes dormant. The only visible trees are evergreens, standing strong against the wind and cold.

How Climate and Elevation Shape the Park's Vegetation

Glacier's plants grow where conditions allow.

- **West vs. East:** The **west side** gets more moisture, leading to thick forests and moss-covered trees. The **east side** is drier, with more open landscapes and hardy, wind-resistant trees.

- **High vs. Low Elevations:** Lower elevations support tall forests, while higher up, trees become smaller and more spaced out. At the highest points, only low-growing plants like mosses and wildflowers survive.

- **Climate Change:** As glaciers melt and temperatures rise, tree lines are creeping higher, and some species, like whitebark pine, are disappearing from areas where they once thrived.

CONSERVATION EFFORTS

Glacier National Park isn't just a breathtaking landscape of towering peaks, ancient forests, and crystal-clear lakes—it's a delicate ecosystem facing real challenges. From climate change to human impact, the park is constantly evolving, and dedicated conservation efforts are working to keep it wild for generations to come.

Whether it's restoring whitebark pine forests, protecting grizzly bears, or slowing glacial retreat, these efforts rely on a mix of science, Indigenous knowledge, and visitor responsibility. Here's how you can be part of the solution.

Saving the Whitebark Pine: A Tree Worth Fighting For

If you've ever hiked Glacier's high-elevation trails, you've likely seen the whitebark pine—sturdy, twisted trees that thrive in the harsh alpine environment. But these trees are under attack from an invasive disease called white pine blister rust, which has wiped out huge numbers of them.

The park, in partnership with the U.S. Forest Service and conservation groups, is working to plant rust-resistant seedlings to keep the species alive. These trees aren't just beautiful—they provide food for grizzly bears and habitat for Clark's nutcrackers.

Want to help? Visitors can volunteer to plant trees or donate to conservation funds dedicated to restoring whitebark pine forests.

Protecting Wildlife: Grizzlies, Goats, and More

One of the biggest draws of Glacier is its incredible wildlife—grizzly bears, mountain goats, moose, and wolverines all call this place home. But as more people visit, the risk to these animals grows. That's why the park enforces strict wildlife rules, like keeping at least 100 yards away from bears and 25 yards from other animals.

Grizzly bear conservation has been a success story, with numbers rebounding thanks to careful management. But keeping bears wild means reducing human encounters—so store food properly, carry bear spray, and respect their space. It's simple: when you keep your distance, you help protect them.

Climate Change and Vanishing Glaciers

Glacier National Park is famous for, well, glaciers. But they're disappearing fast. Since the late 1800s, more than 80% of the park's glaciers have melted due to rising temperatures. That's bad news for the park's entire ecosystem, from alpine plants to cold-water fish.

Scientists are tracking these changes, and visitors can help by joining the **Repeat Photography Project**— snapping photos of glaciers from the same spots as historic images to document their retreat. It's a simple but powerful way to contribute to climate research while enjoying the park.

Leave No Trace: How Visitors Can Help

Everyone who visits Glacier plays a role in conservation. Following **Leave No Trace** principles— staying on trails, packing out trash, and respecting nature—helps protect the park's fragile ecosystem. If you're camping, use bear-resistant food containers and avoid making fires where they aren't allowed.

Want to do more? Join a volunteer program, help restore trails, or pick up litter along the way. Every little action adds up.

The Blackfeet Nation's Role in Conservation

The Blackfeet Nation has lived in this region for centuries, and their knowledge of the land is invaluable. Today, they're deeply involved in conservation efforts, bringing traditional ecological practices to modern environmental challenges.

One example is the **Iinnii Initiative**, which has successfully reintroduced bison to Blackfeet lands. This isn't just about restoring a species—it's about reviving an ecosystem that bison once shaped. Visitors can support Blackfeet-led conservation efforts by joining eco-tours, learning about Indigenous land stewardship, and respecting sacred sites within and around the park.

Biggest Threats and the Road Ahead

Glacier's biggest challenges—climate change, habitat loss, and the pressures of increasing tourism—aren't going away anytime soon. Park officials are working on habitat restoration, expanding wildlife corridors, and strengthening environmental policies to keep the park wild. But they can't do it alone.

How You Can Make a Difference

- Follow **Leave No Trace** to keep the park clean and wild.
- Respect wildlife by keeping your distance and storing food properly.
- Join a **citizen science** program, like the Repeat Photography Project.
- Volunteer for restoration projects or donate to conservation programs.
- Support Blackfeet-led eco-tours and conservation initiatives.

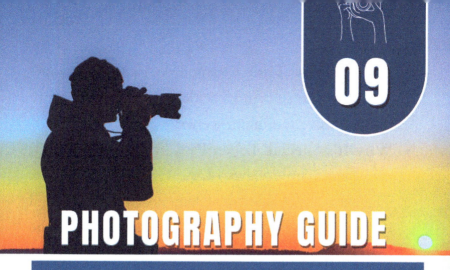

PHOTOGRAPHY GUIDE

BEST SUNRISE AND SUNSET LOCATIONS

Glacier National Park's rugged peaks, crystal-clear lakes, and expansive valleys make it a paradise for photographers chasing the perfect sunrise and sunset. Whether you're looking for golden-hour reflections, alpine glow on mountain ridges, or dramatic cloudscapes, these locations offer some of the most breathtaking views in the park.

Best Sunrise Locations

1. Logan Pass

- **Best Time to Arrive:** At least 30–45 minutes before sunrise
- **Ideal Seasons:** Summer and early fall (June–September)
- **Accessibility:** Drive-in location; parking fills up quickly

- **Photography Tips:** A tripod is essential for low-light conditions; bring a wide-angle lens to capture the expansive mountain scenery
- **Why It's Special:** Logan Pass, sitting at 6,646 feet, offers panoramic views of the Continental Divide. The first light hitting Clements Mountain and Reynolds Mountain creates an incredible alpine glow.

2. Hidden Lake Overlook

- **Best Time to Arrive:** 45 minutes before sunrise
- **Ideal Seasons:** Summer and early fall
- **Accessibility:** 1.5-mile moderate hike from Logan Pass parking lot
- **Photography Tips:** Use a polarizing filter to cut glare from the lake; a telephoto lens helps capture mountain goats and bighorn sheep
- **Why It's Special:** This overlook provides a stunning vantage point of Hidden Lake, with Bearhat Mountain reflecting golden hues during sunrise.

3. Many Glacier (Swiftcurrent Lake & Grinnell Point)

- **Best Time to Arrive:** 30 minutes before sunrise
- **Ideal Seasons:** Spring, summer, and fall

- **Accessibility:** Drive-in location
- **Photography Tips:** Use a graduated ND filter to balance the bright sky and darker landscape; a long exposure can enhance water reflections
- **Why It's Special:** The mirror-like waters of Swiftcurrent Lake beautifully reflect Grinnell Point and the surrounding peaks bathed in soft morning light.

4. Two Medicine Lake

- **Best Time to Arrive:** 30–45 minutes before sunrise
- **Ideal Seasons:** Late spring to fall
- **Accessibility:** Drive-in location with short walks along the shore
- **Photography Tips:** A wide-angle lens is ideal for capturing the entire lake and mountain reflection
- **Why It's Special:** Less crowded than Many Glacier or Logan Pass, Two Medicine offers a serene atmosphere with rising mist and tranquil waters reflecting Sinopah Mountain.

Best Sunset Locations

1. Lake McDonald

- **Best Time to Arrive:** 60 minutes before sunset
- **Ideal Seasons:** Year-round
- Accessibility: Drive-in location with multiple pullouts

- **Photography Tips:** Use a tripod for long exposures; try a telephoto lens to capture alpenglow on distant peaks
- **Why It's Special:** The iconic colorful pebbles, calm waters, and rugged peaks in the background make Lake McDonald one of the most picturesque sunset locations in the park.

2. Apgar Village & Apgar Lookout

- **Best Time to Arrive:** 45 minutes before sunset
- **Ideal Seasons:** Summer and fall
- **Accessibility:** Drive-in location for the village; moderate 3.3-mile hike for the lookout
- **Photography Tips:** A neutral density filter helps smooth water reflections; wide-angle shots work well for capturing the full scope of the sunset
- **Why It's Special:** The Apgar area provides unobstructed views of Lake McDonald with the setting sun painting the sky in fiery oranges and pinks.

3. Big Bend on Going-to-the-Sun Road

- **Best Time to Arrive:** 45 minutes before sunset
- **Ideal Seasons:** Summer (road access is seasonal)
- **Accessibility:** Drive-in location with roadside pullouts

- **Photography Tips:** Use a graduated ND filter for dynamic sky contrast; a telephoto lens works great for distant peaks
- **Why It's Special:** This hairpin turn provides sweeping mountain views, often with dramatic clouds rolling in as the sun dips below the peaks.

4. Bowman Lake

- **Best Time to Arrive:** 1 hour before sunset
- **Ideal Seasons:** Late spring to early fall
- **Accessibility:** Requires a long dirt road drive; limited amenities
- **Photography Tips:** A wide-angle lens captures the entire lake, while a telephoto lens helps with wildlife photography
- **Why It's Special:** One of Glacier's most remote and peaceful lakes, Bowman offers untouched reflections and a chance to capture wildlife in golden light.

Lesser-Known Photography Gems

1. Rising Sun at St. Mary Lake
   - **Why It's Special:** Less crowded than Many Glacier, this area offers stunning sunrise reflections with Wild Goose Island adding a unique focal point.
   - **Tip:** Arrive early to set up at the viewpoint before tour buses arrive.

2. Avalanche Lake at Sunset
   - **Why It's Special:** The lake's still waters create striking mirror-like reflections of the surrounding cliffs and waterfalls.
   - **Tip:** Bring a headlamp for the hike back after sunset.

3. Siyeh Bend at Sunrise
   - **Why It's Special:** Offers lesser-known but dramatic views of Logan Pass with colorful wildflowers in summer.
   - **Tip:** Great for moody misty shots on cloudy mornings.

Seasonal Photo Opportunities

Spring: Waterfalls, Wildlife, and Melting Snow (April – June)

Spring in Glacier is a season of transition, where the last remnants of winter give way to rushing waterfalls and the return of wildlife.

📷 Top Photography Subjects:

- Waterfalls at peak flow: Snowmelt swells the park's waterfalls, making now the best time to capture them. Try Virginia Falls, Running Eagle Falls, and Red Rock Falls.
- Emerging wildlife: Bears, elk, and moose become more active. Spot grizzly bears along Many Glacier Road and black bears near Lake McDonald.
- Snow-capped peaks with fresh greenery: As lower elevations thaw, they create a striking contrast with the snow-draped mountains.

🎯 Hidden Gem: Many Glacier Hotel remains closed until late June, meaning fewer visitors in the area. Capture the reflections of thawing Swiftcurrent Lake before the summer crowds arrive.

🔍 Pro Tip: Use a polarizing filter to cut glare from water and emphasize textures in waterfalls and melting ice.

Summer: Wildflowers, Alpine Reflections, and Clear Skies (July – September)

This is Glacier's busiest season, but it's also when the park is most accessible. Snow-free trails lead to high-alpine views, and lakes reflect the grandeur of the mountains.

📸 **Top Photography Subjects:**

- **Wildflowers in bloom:** Logan Pass bursts with beargrass, Indian paintbrush, and glacier lilies. Take Hidden Lake Overlook Trail or Iceberg Lake Trail for colorful meadows.

- **Crystal-clear reflections:** Early morning shots of Lake McDonald, Swiftcurrent Lake, and Two Medicine Lake yield glassy reflections of the peaks.

- **Milky Way over the mountains:** Glacier's dark skies make it an ideal place for astrophotography. Best spots: Logan Pass and Bowman Lake.

🎯 **Hidden Gem:** Head to **Scenic Point Trail in Two Medicine** for a less-traveled but spectacular view of the St. Mary Valley and surrounding peaks.

🔍 **Pro Tip:** Sunrise and sunset offer the best lighting, with alpenglow illuminating the mountains. Plan your shots around golden hour for softer, more dramatic tones.

Autumn: Fiery Foliage, Wildlife, and Golden Larches (Late September – October)

Fall is a dream season for photographers who want striking colors without summer crowds. The crisp air enhances visibility, and wildlife prepares for winter.

📷 **Top Photography Subjects:**

- **Golden larches:** Unlike evergreen pines, larch trees turn a stunning yellow before shedding their needles. Best locations: North Fork Road, Bowman Lake, and the Highline Trail.
- **Elk rut season:** Capture powerful scenes of bugling elk in the Many Glacier and Two Medicine areas.
- **Red and orange foliage:** St. Mary Valley and Two Medicine Lake showcase some of the best fall colors.

🎯 **Hidden Gem:** Drive **Camas Road** for a scenic fall foliage route with little traffic, offering breathtaking views of aspens and larches.

🔍 **Pro Tip:** Overcast days enhance fall colors by reducing harsh contrast. Use a lower ISO and shoot in RAW to capture the subtle details.

Winter: Snowy Peaks, Frozen Lakes, and Serene Landscapes (November – March)

Winter transforms Glacier into a remote, icy wonderland. While much of the park is inaccessible by car, those willing to hike or ski will find solitude and stunning landscapes.

📷 **Top Photography Subjects:**

- **Snow-covered mountains:** Logan Pass and Going-to-the-Sun Road (closed beyond Avalanche Creek) offer dramatic, snow-draped peaks.
- **Frozen lakes and waterfalls:** Lake McDonald and Two Medicine Lake freeze over, creating unique icy textures.
- **Backcountry beauty:** Snowshoe or cross-country ski into Avalanche Lake for winter solitude.

🎯 **Hidden Gem:** Visit **Lake McDonald Lodge in winter** for a rare chance to photograph the grand hotel covered in snow, free from tourists.

🔍 **Pro Tip:** Cold temperatures drain batteries quickly—carry spares in an inner pocket to keep them warm.

PHOTOGRAPHY TIPS AND ETHICS

Technical Tips: Best Settings for Glacier's Landscapes, Wildlife, and Night Skies

Landscapes:

- **Aperture:** Use a small aperture (f/8–f/16) for greater depth of field, ensuring both foreground and background remain sharp.
- **ISO:** Keep ISO low (100–400) to minimize noise and maintain crisp details.
- **Shutter Speed:** Use a tripod and slower shutter speed for long-exposure shots, especially when photographing waterfalls or clouds moving over peaks.
- **Filters:** A circular polarizer enhances the blues of glacial lakes and cuts glare, while a neutral density (ND) filter helps create silky water effects in rivers and waterfalls.

Wildlife:

- **Aperture:** A wider aperture (f/5.6–f/8) isolates the subject and provides a pleasing background blur (bokeh).
- **Shutter Speed:** Fast shutter speeds (1/500s or higher) are crucial for capturing moving animals like bears or mountain goats.

- **ISO:** Adjust as needed based on lighting conditions, especially in early morning or dusk when wildlife is most active.
- **Lens:** A telephoto lens (300mm or longer) is ideal for safely capturing wildlife from a distance.

Night Photography:

- **Aperture:** Use the widest aperture possible (f/2.8-f/4) to allow more light into the sensor.
- **ISO:** Start at ISO 1600-3200 and adjust based on exposure.
- **Shutter Speed:** 15-25 seconds is ideal for capturing the Milky Way without excessive star trails.
- **Tripod & Remote Shutter:** A stable tripod and remote trigger minimize camera shake for sharper images.

Wildlife Photography: Ethical Practices and Best Locations

Keeping a Safe Distance

Glacier is home to grizzly bears, black bears, moose, mountain goats, and elk. Always stay at least **100 yards from bears and wolves** and **25 yards from other wildlife**. Bring a telephoto lens instead of moving closer.

Best Times & Locations for Wildlife Photography

- **Early morning and late evening** are the best times for spotting wildlife, as animals are more active during these cooler hours.
- **Many Glaciers and Two Medicine**: Great spots for moose and bears near lakes and dense forests.
- **Logan Pass**: Mountain goats and bighorn sheep frequent the area, especially around Hidden Lake Overlook.
- **Many Glacier Road and Camas Road**: Often have bear sightings along the roadside.
- **Polebridge & North Fork**: Quieter areas where you may encounter elusive species like wolverines or lynx.

Crowd Management: Finding Solitude and Hidden Gems

Glacier's popular photography spots can get crowded, especially in summer. Here's how to capture stunning shots without the crowds:

- **Visit at Sunrise or Sunset:** The golden hours provide the best light and fewer people at iconic spots like Lake McDonald, Hidden Lake, and St. Mary Lake.

- **Explore Lesser-Known Locations:**
  - **Bowman Lake & Kintla Lake** (North Fork area) offer stunning reflections with fewer visitors.
  - **Red Rock Falls** (Many Glacier) is a short hike with beautiful cascades and fewer crowds.
  - **Scenic Point** (Two Medicine) provides panoramic views without the rush of tourists.
- **Use Alternative Viewpoints:** Instead of parking at the main Logan Pass lot, hike a bit further for unique perspectives away from crowds.

Weather Challenges: Handling Glacier's Unpredictable Conditions

Glacier's weather is notoriously unpredictable. Sudden storms, high winds, and temperature swings can impact your shoot. Be prepared:

- **Protect Your Gear:** Use rain covers for your camera and keep silica gel packets in your bag to absorb moisture.
- **Dress in Layers:** Mornings and evenings can be chilly, even in summer. Waterproof gear is essential.
- **Check Conditions Before Heading Out:** Weather can change rapidly, so monitor forecasts and carry extra batteries, as cold temperatures drain them faster.

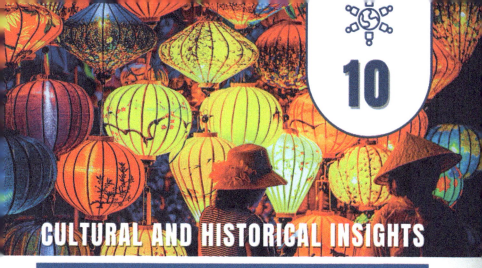

CULTURAL AND HISTORICAL INSIGHTS

INDIGENOUS HERITAGE

Glacier National Park is more than just a breathtaking landscape of rugged mountains, pristine lakes, and expansive valleys—it is a land deeply rooted in the cultural heritage and traditions of the Indigenous peoples who have called it home for thousands of years. Long before it became a national park, this land was part of the ancestral territories of the Blackfeet, Salish, Kootenai, and Pend d'Oreille tribes. Their stories, spiritual beliefs, and conservation practices continue to shape the park's legacy today.

The Land's Significance to Indigenous Tribes

The lands that now comprise Glacier National Park have long been regarded as sacred by the Blackfeet Nation on the east side and the Salish, Kootenai, and Pend d'Oreille peoples to the west.

The Blackfeet refer to the area as the "Backbone of the World," a place of great spiritual power where the natural world and the supernatural are deeply intertwined. Meanwhile, the Salish and Kootenai trace their ancestors to the mountains and valleys of the park, where they engaged in seasonal hunting, gathering, and ceremonies.

The park's towering peaks, shimmering waters, and alpine meadows are woven into Indigenous creation stories. Many sites hold spiritual significance, such as Chief Mountain, a sacred site for the Blackfeet and other Plains tribes. This striking peak has long been a place for vision quests and prayer, a tradition that continues today.

Stories, Traditions, and Spiritual Significance

Indigenous oral traditions speak of the origins of the land, the spirits that inhabit it, and the lessons passed down through generations. Many Blackfeet legends tell of Napi, the Old Man, a trickster and creator figure who shaped the landscape. The Salish and Kootenai share stories of how their ancestors lived in harmony with the land, following the seasonal movements of bison, elk, and other wildlife while respecting the balance of nature.

These traditions influence Indigenous conservation ethics, emphasizing respect, reciprocity, and sustainability.

Indigenous communities continue to practice their cultural traditions, including drumming, storytelling, and sacred ceremonies in and around the park.

Exploring Indigenous Heritage Near Glacier National Park

For visitors eager to learn about the Indigenous cultures that have shaped Glacier National Park, several locations and experiences offer an immersive connection to their heritage:

- **Blackfeet Heritage Center (Browning, MT)** – This cultural center and gallery showcases the history, art, and traditions of the Blackfeet Nation. Visitors can explore exhibits featuring traditional crafts, historical artifacts, and contemporary Blackfeet artists' work.

- **Museum of the Plains Indian (Browning, MT)** – Operated by the U.S. Department of the Interior, this museum provides a deeper dive into the material culture of the Plains tribes, including intricate beadwork, regalia, and historical narratives.

- **Guided Blackfeet Cultural Tours** – Several Blackfeet guides offer cultural interpretive tours, sharing Indigenous perspectives on the landscape, local wildlife, and historic events. These tours often include visits to significant sites such as Two Medicine and Chief Mountain.

- **The People's Center (Pablo, MT)** – Located on the Flathead Reservation, this museum and cultural center provides insights into the traditions of the Salish, Kootenai, and Pend d'Oreille tribes through exhibits, storytelling sessions, and demonstrations of traditional crafts.

Indigenous Knowledge and Conservation Practices

For thousands of years, Indigenous tribes managed the land using traditional ecological knowledge, which emphasized sustainable hunting, controlled burns, and respect for the natural cycles of wildlife and plant life. This knowledge continues to influence modern conservation efforts. Today, tribal biologists and land managers collaborate with the National Park Service to protect the park's ecosystems.

Efforts such as bison restoration projects, native plant conservation, and wildfire management reflect Indigenous practices that have long safeguarded the land's health. Tribal perspectives also inform wildlife conservation initiatives, particularly regarding wolves, grizzly bears, and other keystone species.

Ongoing Tribal Efforts to Preserve Heritage

Indigenous communities continue to fight for the recognition and preservation of their cultural sites within Glacier National Park.

The Blackfeet Nation remains actively involved in park-related discussions, advocating for the protection of sacred places and traditional practices. Annual events such as powwows, cultural festivals, and storytelling gatherings help maintain and share their heritage.

Additionally, partnerships between tribal governments and federal agencies are working to improve the representation of Indigenous history within the park's interpretive programs, ensuring that visitors gain a fuller understanding of the park's deep cultural roots.

Practical Tips for Visitors

- **Respect Indigenous Lands** – Many sacred sites near Glacier National Park, such as Chief Mountain, hold spiritual significance. Visitors should observe these places with respect and avoid disturbing cultural landmarks.

- **Attend a Cultural Event** – Check local event calendars in Browning and on the Flathead Reservation for cultural festivals, powwows, and storytelling gatherings.

- **Support Indigenous-Owned Businesses** – Consider purchasing art, crafts, and goods from Indigenous artists and businesses, such as those found at the Blackfeet Heritage Center.

Going-to-the-Sun Road: A Masterpiece of Mountain Engineering

One of the most famous roads in the world, **Going-to-the-Sun Road** is a 50-mile engineering marvel that carves through the heart of Glacier National Park. Built between 1921 and 1932, this winding, high-elevation road was a daring endeavor, with workers using dynamite and hand tools to carve a path through sheer cliffs. Today, it stands as a **National Historic Landmark**, offering some of the most spectacular views in North America.

◆ **How to Experience It**: Drive or take the park's shuttle (summer only) to soak in breathtaking scenery. Logan Pass, the road's highest point, offers excellent hiking and wildlife viewing.

◆ **Tip**: Portions of the road close due to snow, sometimes until early July. Check conditions before your trip.

Historic Chalets and Lodges: Echoes of Glacier's Golden Era

In the early 1900s, the Great Northern Railway built grand hotels and rustic backcountry chalets to attract adventurous tourists, many of whom arrived by train.

These historic lodges still capture the spirit of Glacier's early tourism boom.

- **Many Glacier Hotel** (1915) – This grand Swiss-style lodge sits on Swiftcurrent Lake, offering stunning mountain views. Guests can stay overnight, dine at the Ptarmigan Dining Room, or explore nearby trails.
- **Sperry Chalet** (1914) – Accessible only by an arduous 6.7-mile hike, this backcountry lodge offers a rare glimpse into Glacier's past. After a devastating fire in 2017, it was meticulously rebuilt and reopened in 2020.
- **Granite Park Chalet** (1914) – Another remote yet rewarding destination, this rustic chalet is perched high in the mountains and is accessible via the **Highline Trail** or the **Loop Trail**.

◆ **How to Experience It**: Reserve well in advance for overnight stays, as these historic lodges fill up quickly. Day hikers can visit the chalets for a break and take in the history.

◆ **Tip**: Many Glacier Hotel is accessible by car, but Sperry and Granite Park require strenuous hikes—plan accordingly.

Indigenous and Early Settler Influence: A Land of Deep Roots

Long before Glacier became a national park, the **Blackfeet, Salish, Kootenai, and Pend d'Oreille** people lived and traveled through these lands, hunting bison, fishing, and trading. The park's landscape is rich with Indigenous history, from sacred sites to places that still hold deep cultural significance.

- **Two Medicine Valley** – A historically significant area for the Blackfeet Nation, this region is home to ancient stories, sacred sites, and stunning scenery.
- **Apikuni Falls** – Named after a Blackfeet warrior and historian, this short hike near Many Glacier offers a chance to reflect on Indigenous history.
- **Old North Trail** – This ancient trade route ran along the Rocky Mountain Front, connecting Indigenous peoples for thousands of years.

◆ **How to Experience It:** Visit the **Museum of the Plains Indian** in nearby Browning, Montana, or attend a Blackfeet cultural event. Interpretive signs at key sites provide insight into Indigenous heritage.

◆ **Tip:** Be respectful of sacred sites and learn about the land's Indigenous history before visiting.

Fire Lookouts and Ranger Stations: Guardians of the Wilderness

Before modern technology, fire lookouts played a crucial role in protecting Glacier's forests. These isolated towers, perched on mountaintops, housed watchmen who scanned the horizon for smoke. Many of these historic structures remain standing today.

- **Huckleberry Fire Lookout** – A challenging 6-mile hike leads to this still-active fire lookout, offering panoramic views over the park.
- **Swiftcurrent Fire Lookout** – Perched high above **Swiftcurrent Pass**, this remote lookout rewards hikers with incredible vistas of the Many Glacier region.
- **Belton Bridge and Historic Ranger Station** – Located near West Glacier, this site served as an early gateway to the park and remains a historical point of interest.

◆ **How to Experience It**: Hike to the lookouts for a glimpse into the past and unmatched views. The Belton Bridge area is easily accessible by car for those seeking a historic stop without the climb.

◆ **Tip**: Fire lookouts require long hikes with significant elevation gain—be prepared with water, snacks, and proper gear.

PARK MUSEUMS AND EXHIBITS

Apgar & St. Mary Visitor Centers – Gateway to Glacier's Past and Present

Apgar Visitor Center (West Entrance)

📍 **Location:** Near West Glacier, close to Apgar Village

⏳ **Best Time to Visit:** Open daily in summer, limited hours in winter

💡 **Why Visit?** A great first stop for orientation and interactive exhibits

Apgar Visitor Center serves as an essential introduction to Glacier's landscape and history. Here, visitors can explore displays about the park's diverse wildlife, fire ecology, and the formation of its signature glacial valleys. Large maps and topographic models help explain the terrain, and rangers are available to provide hiking recommendations and safety tips. If you're interested in seeing how climate change affects the park, interactive exhibits track the retreat of glaciers over time—an eye-opening look at the park's evolving landscape.

Visitor Tip: This is a great place to pick up a Junior Ranger booklet for kids, grab trail maps, and check current road and weather conditions before setting out on your adventure.

St. Mary Visitor Center (East Entrance)

📍 **Location:** Near the east entrance of Going-to-the-Sun Road

⏳ **Best Time to Visit:** Open seasonally (primarily summer and fall)

💡 **Why Visit?** Features excellent exhibits on Blackfeet culture and the park's geology

St. Mary Visitor Center provides an immersive introduction to both the natural and cultural history of Glacier. Unlike Apgar, this center focuses more on the indigenous connections to the land, particularly those of the Blackfeet Nation, whose ancestral territory includes much of the park's eastern landscape. Exhibits feature Blackfeet oral histories, traditional art, and artifacts that showcase the deep relationship between the tribe and the land.

A highlight here is the **park film**, which tells the story of Glacier's landscapes and its people through breathtaking cinematography and Blackfeet perspectives.

Visitor Tip: Rangers at St. Mary often lead short interpretive walks that explore the connections between the Blackfeet and Glacier's natural resources—well worth the time if you're interested in indigenous history.

Museum of the Plains Indian – A Deeper Dive into Blackfeet Heritage

📍 **Location:** Browning, MT (about 30 minutes from the park's east entrance)

⏳ **Best Time to Visit:** Open year-round (hours vary seasonally)

💡 **Why Visit?** A rich collection of Blackfeet and Plains Indian art and history

While not inside the park, the **Museum of the Plains Indian** in Browning is a must-visit for those who want a deeper understanding of the Blackfeet Nation and other Plains tribes. The museum houses an impressive collection of historical and contemporary indigenous art, intricate beadwork, traditional clothing, and ceremonial items. Life-size dioramas depict the daily life of Plains Indians, from buffalo hunting to sacred ceremonies, providing a vivid glimpse into traditions that continue today.

One of the most powerful sections of the museum tells the story of the Blackfeet's connection to the land that is now Glacier National Park and how government policies affected their access to their ancestral homeland.

Visitor Tip: Pair your visit with a stop at the Blackfeet Heritage Center nearby for more locally made art and cultural experiences.

Ranger Talks & Programs – Bringing Glacier's History to Life

📍 **Locations:** Throughout the park, including visitor centers, lodges, and popular trailheads

⏳ **Best Time to Visit:** Summer (check the park's website for schedules)

💡 **Why Attend?** A chance to hear stories from experts and see history come alive

Glacier's seasonal **ranger-led programs** are one of the best ways to experience the park's rich history up close. From fireside chats in the historic lodges to guided history walks along famous trails, these programs provide fascinating insights into the park's past.

Popular programs include:

- **Blackfeet History Walks** (offered at St. Mary) – Led by tribal members, these walks explore the traditional relationship between the Blackfeet and Glacier's landscape.
- **Historic Chalets & Trails Tours** – Learn about the original backcountry chalets and the rugged journeys early visitors took to reach them.
- **Wildlife & Conservation Talks** – Hear about the early efforts to protect Glacier's grizzlies, mountain goats, and other wildlife.

Visitor Tip: These talks are free and don't require reservations, but they do fill up quickly—arrive early to get a good spot!

DINING AND SUPPLIES

In-Park Dining Options

Planning your dining experiences in Glacier National Park can enhance your visit, ensuring you're well-fed and ready for adventure. Here's a practical guide to the in-park dining options, along with insider tips to make the most of your culinary journey.

Many Glacier Area

- **Ptarmigan Dining Room**: Located within the Many Glacier Hotel, this dining room offers breakfast, lunch, and dinner with a focus on regional Montana cuisine. The atmosphere is rustic and cozy, reflecting the hotel's historic charm.

- **Insider Tip**: Arrive early for dinner to secure a window seat overlooking Swiftcurrent Lake. Reservations are not accepted, so early arrival helps avoid peak dining times.

- **'Nell's at Swiftcurrent Motor Inn**: A casual spot known for its quick-service meals, including pizza, burgers, and local beers on tap. It's a favorite among hikers looking for a hearty meal after a day on the trails.
- **Insider Tip**: The pizza, while simple, is especially satisfying after a long hike. Service is on a first-come, first-served basis, so plan accordingly.
- **Heidi's Snack Shop & Espresso Stand**: Perfect for a quick bite or caffeine boost, offering snacks, sandwiches, and espresso beverages.
- **Insider Tip**: Ideal for early risers needing a light breakfast before hitting the trails. Lines can form quickly in the morning.

Lake McDonald Area

- **Russell's Fireside Dining Room**: Situated in Lake McDonald Lodge, this dining room serves breakfast, lunch, and dinner with a menu highlighting Montana-inspired dishes. The ambiance is reminiscent of a hunting lodge, complete with lake views.
- **Insider Tip**: No reservations are accepted, so consider dining during off-peak hours to avoid waits.

- **Jammer Joe's Grill & Pizzeria**: Offers family-friendly dining with a menu featuring pizzas, pasta, salads, and sandwiches. It's a convenient option for a casual meal.
- **Insider Tip**: Open for lunch and dinner from 11:30 AM to 9 PM. It's a good choice for families or groups looking for a quick meal.
- **Lucke's Lounge**: Adjacent to Russell's, this lounge provides a relaxed setting with a menu of small bites and beverages, perfect for unwinding after a day of exploration.
- **Insider Tip**: Open from 11:30 AM to 9:30 PM, it's a great spot for a late lunch or evening drink.

Rising Sun Area

- **Two Dog Flats Grill**: Located at Rising Sun Motor Inn, this grill offers breakfast, lunch, and dinner with a focus on local specialties and seasonal offerings.
- **Insider Tip**: The huckleberry pancakes are a breakfast favorite. Operating hours are typically from 6:30 AM to 9:30 PM, but it's best to check current schedules.

Apgar Village

- **Eddie's Café & Mercantile**: A family-owned establishment serving breakfast, lunch, and dinner. The menu includes omelets, burgers, wraps, and homemade pies.
- **Insider Tip**: Breakfast is served until 11:15 AM, and the café closes at 9 PM. It's also a convenient spot to pick up souvenirs or camping supplies.

General Tips for Dining in Glacier National Park

- **Operating Hours**: Most dining facilities operate seasonally, typically from late June through September. Always verify current hours before planning your meals.
- **Reservations**: In-park restaurants generally do not accept reservations. To avoid long waits, consider dining during off-peak hours, such as early lunch or late dinner.
- **Crowd Management**: Arriving early, especially for dinner, can help secure preferable seating and reduce wait times.
- **Alternative Options**: While the park has several dining facilities, options can be limited, especially for those with dietary restrictions. Consider bringing supplemental food items or exploring dining options in nearby towns like West Glacier or St. Mary.

GROCERY STORES AND MARKETS

Whether you're camping, staying at a lodge, or just passing through, knowing where to grab groceries and supplies in Glacier National Park is essential. You won't find massive supermarkets inside the park, but there are a handful of general stores offering basic necessities. If you're looking for fresh produce, specialty items, or affordable groceries, the best bet is stopping in one of the nearby towns before heading into the park.

After a few trips to Glacier, I've learned the hard way that stocking up ahead of time saves both money and frustration—so here's everything you need to know about where to shop, what to buy, and a few insider tips to make your trip smoother.

In-Park Stores – Limited but Useful

Glacier's in-park stores are convenient for last-minute essentials, but they're small and often overpriced. Think granola bars, trail mix, canned goods, and a limited selection of drinks. If you forgot toothpaste or need a souvenir, they've got you covered. If you want fresh produce, a wide variety of snacks, or full meal ingredients, you'll need to go outside the park.

Apgar Village Store (West Entrance)

📍 *Located in Apgar Village, near Lake McDonald*

This is the best-stocked general store in the park, and it has a little bit of everything: snacks, camping supplies, drinks, and souvenirs. They also have firewood if campfires are permitted during your visit. Expect high prices, but if you're in a pinch, it's a solid stop.

📝 **Insider Tip:** If you're grabbing food for a day hike, they carry pre-made sandwiches and some fresh fruit. But they go fast—by mid-morning, the selection is slim.

Lake McDonald Camp Store

📍 *Near Lake McDonald Lodge*

This is a tiny shop mostly catering to lodge guests and campers. You'll find packaged snacks, beer, ice, and some camping gear. If you need something like batteries or bug spray, they'll likely have it, but don't expect a full grocery selection.

📝 **Insider Tip:** If you're staying in the area for multiple days and want decent coffee in the morning, grab a bag of Montana Coffee Traders coffee here—it's locally roasted and way better than instant coffee from your campsite.

Many Glacier Hotel & Camp Store (Many Glacier Area)

📍 *Inside Many Glacier Hotel & another store near Swiftcurrent Motor Inn*

These are the last places to grab supplies before heading out on trails like Grinnell Glacier or Iceberg Lake. The selection is small—mostly snacks, canned food, and a few drinks.

📝 **Insider Tip:** The best thing about this store? The huckleberry chocolate bars. Grab one. You'll thank me later.

Grocery Stores in Nearby Towns – Where You Should Really Stock Up

If you want real grocery shopping options with fresh food, you'll need to stop in one of the towns outside the park. Here's where to go:

West Glacier (Closest to West Entrance)

- West Glacier Mercantile – A small store with the basics, including ice, drinks, and pre-made sandwiches. It's better than the in-park stores but still pricey.

- **Glacier View Market (Coram, 7 min from West Glacier)** – A small but well-stocked market with fresh produce, deli meats, and even organic options.

🖍 **Insider Tip:** If you need ice, grab it here—it's cheaper than inside the park and melts slower than the flimsy bags from the gas stations.

Columbia Falls (Best Grocery Options Before Entering from West)

- **Super 1 Foods** – This is where I always stop before heading into the park. It's a full grocery store with everything you'd find at home, plus a good bakery and deli.
- **Smith's Food and Drug** – Another solid option, great for grabbing fresh meat or specialty items.

🖍 **Insider Tip:** If you're camping and need a cooler, this is the place to buy one. Glacier's general stores carry them, but you'll pay double.

Whitefish (More Variety, Best for Specialty Foods)

- **Third Street Market** – If you want organic, local, or specialty foods, this is the best place. They carry fresh local produce and even bison and elk meat.
- **Super 1 Foods (again, but bigger)** – Great selection, and often less busy than the Columbia Falls location.

Insider Tip: If you're a coffee lover, stop by Montana Coffee Traders in Whitefish and grab a bag of their locally roasted beans. It beats anything you'll find in the park.

St. Mary (Closest to East Entrance, Limited Selection)

- **St. Mary Grocery Store** – The best option on the east side of the park. They carry produce, meat, and most of what you'd need for a camping trip.
- **Duck Lake Lodge Store** – More of a convenience store but has snacks, beer, and ice.

Insider Tip: If you're planning to hike in the Many Glacier area, this is your last chance to grab fresh food before options become extremely limited.

Specialty Food Shops – Huckleberry Everything

If you want a true taste of Montana, these places are worth a stop:

- The Huckleberry Patch (Hungry Horse) – The go-to place for all things huckleberry: jams, syrups, candies, even huckleberry fudge.
- Polebridge Mercantile (North Fork Area) – Famous for its huckleberry bear claws, this historic bakery is a must-stop if you're headed toward Bowman Lake.

Insider Tip: If you plan on buying huckleberry syrup as a souvenir, get it here. The bottles inside the park are way more expensive.

Gas Stations with Convenience Stores – Quick & Easy Stops

If you just need snacks, drinks, or fuel, here are the best gas station stops:

- **West Glacier Gas Station** – Right outside the entrance. Expect high prices but decent selection.
- **Town Pump (Columbia Falls & Whitefish)** – Good for grabbing snacks, coffee, and last-minute camping essentials.
- **Sinclair Gas Station (St. Mary)** – Open 24/7, which is rare in this area.

✏️ **Insider Tip:** If you're road-tripping through Montana, Town Pump gas stations usually have the cheapest fuel compared to others in the area.

PICNIC AREAS

Best Picnic Areas in Glacier National Park

Glacier National Park is one of those places where a picnic isn't just a meal—it's an experience. Whether you're looking for a quiet lakeside retreat, a mountain backdrop, or a chance to spot wildlife, there's a perfect picnic spot for you. But, if there's one thing I've learned from past trips, it's that a little planning makes all the difference. The best spots fill up fast, and bear safety is a must. Here's my guide to the most scenic picnic areas in the park, plus some insider tips to make your meal unforgettable.

1. Apgar Picnic Area – Lakeside Views & Easy Access

📍 Near Apgar Village, West Glacier

If you want a picnic spot with easy access and a gorgeous view, Apgar Picnic Area is the place to be. Located right by Lake McDonald, this area has picnic tables, restrooms, and fire grates. It's also one of the easiest picnic areas to get to, making it a great choice for families or anyone who doesn't want to trek far with a cooler.

📝 **Insider Tip:** *Get there early, especially in summer.* The parking lot fills up fast, especially between 11 AM and 2 PM. If you grab a spot early, you can enjoy a peaceful morning picnic while the lake is still calm.

🔥 **Restrictions:** *Campfires are often banned in summer due to fire danger, so bring a portable stove if you plan to cook.*

2. Sprague Creek Picnic Area – Shaded & Secluded

📍 *North Shore of Lake McDonald*

This little gem is just off the Going-to-the-Sun Road, but it's far enough from the main parking areas to feel secluded. The picnic tables here are shaded by tall trees, making it a great spot on hot summer days. You're also right by the lake, so you can take a post-lunch stroll along the shore.

📝 **Insider Tip:** *If you're driving west on Going-to-the-Sun Road, this is one of the last good picnic spots before hitting the busy Apgar area. Stop here if you want a quieter meal.*

🔥 **Restrictions:** *No campfires allowed. Pack out all trash to keep the area pristine.*

3. Two Medicine Picnic Area – Fewer Crowds, Stunning Views

📍 *Two Medicine Lake, East Glacier*

If you're looking for a picnic spot away from the crowds, Two Medicine is perfect. It's about an hour's drive from the main park entrances, but that means fewer people and some of the best scenery in the park. The picnic area sits near the lake, with dramatic mountain peaks in the background.

📝 **Insider Tip:** *This is one of the best places for a sunset picnic. Most day hikers leave by late afternoon, leaving you with a peaceful, postcard-perfect view.*

🔥 **Restrictions:** *Fire pits available, but fire bans are common. Check for restrictions before you go.*

4. Many Glacier Picnic Areas – Wildlife & Waterfalls

📍 *Near Swiftcurrent Lake, Many Glacier*

Many Glacier is known for its incredible wildlife, and the picnic areas here put you right in the middle of it. There are several spots with picnic tables near the Many Glacier Hotel and Swiftcurrent Motor Inn, as well as some more hidden spots along the lake. If you're lucky, you might spot moose or bears from a safe distance.

📝 **Insider Tip:** *Bring binoculars! I've spotted grizzly bears grazing on distant hills while having lunch here. If you're planning to hike Grinnell Glacier, this is a great place for a pre- or post-hike meal.*

🔥 **Restrictions:** *No unattended food—this is prime bear country. Use the provided bear-proof storage lockers.*

Packing the Perfect Picnic in Glacier

If you're heading out for a picnic in the park, here's what I've learned to pack over the years:

✅ **Bear-Safe Food Storage** – Always keep food in a bear-proof container or your car when not eating. Never leave it unattended.

✅ **Cold Drinks & Ice Packs** – Most picnic areas don't have running water, so bring plenty of drinks. A frozen water bottle doubles as an ice pack and a cold drink later.

✅ **Huckleberry Snacks** – If you see huckleberry-flavored anything in a local market, grab it. Huckleberry chocolates, dried berries, or jam are a must-try.

✅ **Bug Spray & Sunscreen** – Even in the mountains, the sun is strong, and mosquitos can be relentless.

✅ **Trash Bags** – Many picnic areas are "pack-in, pack-out," meaning you have to take your trash with you.

✅ **Folding Chairs** – Some picnic areas have tables, but if you're heading to Bowman Lake or a remote spot, you'll want your own seating.

✅ **A Blanket** – Not all picnic spots have tables, and some of the best meals are eaten on a lakeside rock with a breathtaking view.

Best Times for a Picnic in Glacier

Timing makes all the difference for a peaceful meal in the park. Here's when to go:

Early Morning (7 AM – 9 AM) – Best for solitude, crisp air, and a quiet start to the day. This is especially great at Lake McDonald or Two Medicine.

Midday **(11 AM – 1 PM)** – The busiest time. If you want a picnic table, arrive before 11 AM.

Late Afternoon (3 PM – 6 PM) – Many day visitors start leaving, making this a quieter window.

Sunset (6 PM – 9 PM in summer) – A magical time for a lakeside picnic. Apgar, Two Medicine, and Bowman Lake are especially beautiful at sunset.

SAFETY AND EMERGENCY INFORMATION

WEATHER CONSIDERATIONS

Glacier National Park Weather & Outdoor Experiences by Season

Spring (April–June): Snow, Rain & Unpredictable Skies

Spring in Glacier feels like winter's stubborn grip refusing to let go. I've started hikes under sunny skies, only to be caught in a sudden snow squall. **Going-to-the-Sun Road? Still buried under feet of snow.** Lower trails around Lake McDonald start melting out, but higher elevations remain inaccessible. Rain, slush, and icy mornings mean waterproof boots and layers are a must. Bears are waking up—so am I, but with bear spray in hand.

Summer (July–September): Warm Days, Wild Storms & Fire Season

If you want the full Glacier experience, **this is it**—but so does everyone else. I've sweated under a blazing sun at Logan Pass, only to be drenched by a fast-moving thunderstorm an hour later. **Wildfires are a real threat**, filling the valleys with smoke some years. Trails are open, waterfalls are raging, and wildlife is everywhere. Start early, carry water, and don't underestimate the altitude—it sneaks up on you.

Fall (October–November): Quiet, Crisp & Unpredictable

This is when Glacier slows down, and I love it. The **Going-to-the-Sun Road closes mid-October**, but the lower trails, dusted with golden larch trees, are stunning. Mornings are **cold, sometimes icy**, and the first real snowstorms can hit anytime. Wildlife is active —elk bugling in the valleys, bears foraging before hibernation. I've learned to carry extra layers and **never trust the weather forecast**—snow has surprised me in October more than once.

Winter (December–March): A Frozen Wilderness

Glaciers in winter feel like stepping into another world —silent, vast, brutally cold.

The road is closed past Avalanche Creek, and deep snow blankets the landscape. I've snowshoed through peaceful forests where the only sound was my breath and the crunch of ice underfoot. Avalanches are a real risk in the backcountry, and temperatures regularly dip below zero. If you're not prepared, **this place will humble you.**

What I've Learned About Glacier's Weather

- **Layer up**—it can go from summer to winter in an hour.
- **Check road & trail conditions**—the park's terrain changes daily.
- **Wildlife is always around**—I've seen bears, goats, and moose when I least expected it.
- **Expect the unexpected**—storms, snow, fires, and cold snaps are all part of the experience.

WILDLIFE ENCOUNTERS

One of the greatest thrills of visiting Glacier National Park is encountering its diverse and often elusive wildlife. From **grizzly bears lumbering through alpine meadows** to **mountain goats effortlessly scaling cliffs**, the park is teeming with iconic species. But with these encounters comes responsibility—both for safety and for preserving the natural habitat.

Wildlife You Might Encounter

Grizzly & Black Bears

Bears are **the most famous residents of Glacier**, and for good reason. The park is home to a **healthy population of grizzlies and black bears**, often spotted along trails, meadows, and even near campgrounds.

- **Grizzly Bears:** Larger with a distinctive shoulder hump, grizzlies are more aggressive if threatened.
- **Black Bears:** Smaller, with no shoulder hump, and can be black, brown, or cinnamon-colored.

Mountain Goats

The **unofficial symbol of Glacier**, these sure-footed climbers are frequently seen at **Logan Pass**, **Highline Trail**, and along rocky cliffs. They may seem docile, but **never get too close**—they have sharp horns and can be unpredictable.

Moose

Moose are **massive and solitary**, often spotted in **wetlands near Fishercap Lake** and **Many Glacier**. Despite their calm appearance, moose can be **aggressive**, especially if startled or with calves.

Wolverines

Among Glacier's most elusive predators, wolverines are **rarely seen** due to their vast territories and reclusive nature. If you're lucky enough to spot one, consider it a once-in-a-lifetime event!

How to Safely Observe Wildlife

Seeing wildlife in their natural environment is a privilege, but it's essential to keep a safe distance and avoid disturbing them.

Safe Viewing Guidelines

- Stay at least 100 yards (91 meters) from bears & wolves.
- Stay at least 25 yards (23 meters) from other animals like moose, mountain goats, and elk.
- Use binoculars or a zoom lens instead of getting closer.
- Do not feed wildlife—this disrupts their natural behavior and endangers both animals and humans.
- Respect trail closures—they are often in place to protect wildlife habitat.

Bear Safety: What You Need to Know

Bears are active throughout the park, especially in the spring and late summer when foraging for food. Understanding bear safety is critical for every visitor.

How to Properly Use Bear Spray

1. **Keep it accessible** (not in your backpack—holster it on your belt).
2. **Know how to use it** before you need it. Remove the safety clip and aim slightly downward.
3. **If a bear charges**, spray in a sweeping motion when it is **30-60 feet away**.
4. **Leave the area after using it**—the residue can attract bears.

Food & Scent Storage

- Store all food in **bear-proof lockers** or **hang food at least 10 feet high and 4 feet from tree trunks** in backcountry sites.
- **Never leave food unattended**—even a candy wrapper can attract bears.
- **Use bear-resistant containers** in bear country.

How to React During a Bear Encounter

- **If you see a bear in the distance**, back away slowly and **do not run**.
- **If a bear approaches**, speak calmly and firmly while slowly backing away.

- **If a bear charges, use bear spray** and **stand your ground**—most charges are bluff charges.
- **If a grizzly bear attacks**, play dead—lie flat on your stomach with your hands behind your neck.
- **If a black bear attacks**, fight back aggressively.

Hiking Smart: Reducing Wildlife Encounters

Best Practices for Hiking in Bear Country

1. **Travel in Groups** – Bears are less likely to approach a group than a solo hiker.
2. **Make Noise** – Clap, call out, or talk loudly to avoid surprising wildlife.
3. **Hike During Daylight** – Bears and other wildlife are most active at dawn and dusk.
4. **Be Aware of Your Surroundings** – Watch for **tracks, scat, and claw marks** on trees.
5. **Carry Bear Spray** – Every hiker should have it and know how to use it.

EMERGENCY CONTACTS AND SERVICES

Glacier National Park's remote wilderness means **help isn't always nearby**, so knowing where to find emergency services and how to seek help is essential for every visitor. **Cell service is limited**, and weather can delay rescue efforts, so preparation is key.

Essential Emergency Contacts

- **Park Emergency Dispatch (24/7):** 📞 911 (or use an emergency call box)
- **Glacier National Park Headquarters:** 📞 (406) 888-7800
- **Park Ranger Station (Non-Emergency):** 📞 (406) 888-7077
- **Flathead County Sheriff's Office:** 📞 (406) 758-5585
- **Search and Rescue (Flathead County):** 📞 (406) 758-5610
- **Nearest Hospitals:**
  - **Logan Health – Whitefish (24/7 ER)** 📞 (406) 863-3500

Logan Health Medical Center – Kalispell (Major Trauma Center) 📞 (406) 752-5111

Ranger Stations & Visitor Centers

Park rangers provide **information, assistance, and emergency aid**. Always check in with a visitor center or ranger station before heading into the backcountry.
Main Visitor Centers

- **Apgar Visitor Center** (West Entrance) – Open year-round, closest to medical services.
- **St. Mary Visitor Center** (East Entrance) – Closest to Many Glacier and Logan Pass.
- **Logan Pass Visitor Center** – Seasonal, at the highest point of **Going-to-the-Sun Road**.
- **Two Medicine & Many Glacier Ranger Stations** – Summer only; staff can assist with emergencies.

First Aid & Medical Services in the Park

Glacier has **no full-service hospitals within the park**. Rangers and first responders provide **basic first aid**, but serious medical emergencies require transport to hospitals in Whitefish or Kalispell.

- First-aid stations are available at **Apgar and St. Mary Visitor Centers**.
- Local **fire & EMS services** respond to incidents along major roads.

Staying Safe in Glacier's Backcountry

Cell service is unreliable in most of the park, especially in Logan Pass, Many Glacier, and Two Medicine.

How to Stay Connected & Call for Help

✓ Carry a physical map – GPS and phones won't always work.

✓ Use satellite messengers (Garmin inReach, SPOT) for remote trips.

✓ Tell someone your itinerary and expected return time.

✓ Check in at a ranger station before heading into the wilderness.

Made in the USA
Coppell, TX
13 April 2025